MW01137731

DANIEL

The Kingdom of the Lord

DANIEL

The Kingdom of the Lord

CHARLES LEE FEINBERG

BMH BOOKS
P.O. Box 544
Winona Lake, Indiana 46590

All Scripture quotations are from the *New American Standard Bible,* © 1960, 1962, 1963, 1968, 1971, 1972, 1973, 1975 by The Lockman Foundation, and are used by permission.

Library of Congress Cataloging in Publication Data
Feinberg, Charles Lee.
  Daniel, The Kingdom of the Lord.
  Bibliography: c.
  1. Bible. O.T. Daniel—Commentaries. I. Title
BS1555.3.F44   224'.5077   80-70117
ISBN: 0-88469-157-8   AACR2
First Edition, Christian Herald Books, 1981
Second Printing, BMH Books, March 1984
Printed in the United States of America

To
J. Richard Chase, Ph.D.,
president of Biola College,
Talbot Theological Seminary,
Rosemead School of Psychology,

Capable scholar,
efficient administrator,
man of God,
considerate friend,

this volume is gratefully
and affectionately dedicated

Contents

Purpose

IT HAS BEEN SAID that authors write books for laymen when they cannot write them for scholars. That is not necessarily true. An overriding motivation can be to follow the example of the Lord Jesus, whom the common people heard gladly.

As for the author, in some fifty years of teaching Old Testament and Semitic languages, he has had numerous opportunities, and availed himself of them, to teach the book of Daniel in the original Hebrew and Aramaic. But there is always room for a new approach to this part of the canon, which has endless attraction for the child of God. Besides, no one has yet written the definitive work on any book of Scripture. We all strive to the edification of the people of God.

Preface

The book of Daniel is of perennial interest and has always been beloved among the people of God. Unfortunately, it is probably safe to say that Christians have esteemed it even more highly than unbelieving Jews, who have not accepted the marvelous fulfillment of its prophecy concerning Messiah's first coming. It is recognized that many volumes have been written with comments on the prophecy. It would be impossible for anyone to expect to write something on this prophecy that would be clearly original.

The basis of this volume was a series of radio messages given on the program known as the "New Standard for Living," a part of the Lockman Bible Ministries. The purpose throughout has been to convey the inner meaning of the book and, at the same time, make it applicable and understandable to the people of God. From the many responses received, both oral and written, it is clear that the Lord has, according to His promise, blessed His Word beyond all our expectations.

Thanks are due Mr. Robert Lambeth, president of the Lockman Foundation, for his encouragement in having the material published. Gratitude is here expressed to those who have worked on the manuscript in the publishing house, and especially to my efficient secretary, Miss Shirley Shively.

We commend the work to the blessing of God and invite comment that would enhance the usefulness of the volume.

Charles Lee Feinberg
Whittier, California

Introduction

The book of Daniel is unquestionably the key to all biblical prophecy. It is the great apocalyptic book of the Old Testament, whereas Revelation is that of the New Testament. Passages such as Matthew 24-25, Mark 13, Luke 21, and the book of Revelation are unintelligible without a knowledge of the book of Daniel.

Daniel is the fourth of the major prophets of the Old Testament:

Isaiah speaks of the *salvation* of the Lord;
Jeremiah speaks of the *judgment* of the Lord;
Ezekiel speaks of the *glory* of the Lord; and
Daniel speaks of the *kingdom* of the Lord,

and that in relation to the "times of the Gentiles" (cf. Rev. 11:15). Contrary to the mistaken belief of many, Daniel can be—and is meant to be—understood (Matt. 24:15). In the words of Sir Isaac Newton, "To reject Daniel is to reject the Christian religion."

The Writer

More is known about the writer of the book of Daniel than about any other prophet. Daniel was a son of the royal line of Judah (Dan. 1:3) who was deported to Babylon in 606 B.C. as a prisoner of King Nebuchadnezzar. He became a close advisor to the king, and although the corruption of court life surrounded him, he kept himself separated to the Lord. Daniel is described in Scripture as a great man of faith, a man characterized by his piety, humility, and dependence upon God (Ezek. 14:14, 20; Dan. 9:20; 10:11; Matt. 24:15; Heb. 11:32-33).

Outline of Daniel

I. *Daniel 1-6. The Dreams of Gentile Rulers*
  A. Chapter 1: The preparation of God's servant
  B. Chapter 2: The consternation of men; and the interpretation of the dream
  C. Chapter 3: The golden image of Nebuchadnezzar
  D. Chapter 4: The vision of the great tree
  E. Chapter 5: The handwriting on the wall
  F. Chapter 6: Daniel in the lions' den

II. *Daniel 7-12. Dreams and Visions of the Last Days*
  A. Chapter 7: The world empires and the little horn
  B. Chapter 8: The vision of the ram and the goat
  C. Chapter 9: The prophecy of the seventy weeks
  D. Chapter 10: The delayed answer to prayer
  E. Chapter 11: The wars of the Ptolemies and the Seleucidae; and the Antichrist
  F. Chapter 12: The time of the end

Historical Background

The study of ancient history reveals that no single power was able to gain absolute control over all others. The Egyptians, the Assyrians, and other empires all attempted total domination, but without success. It was not until Israel had turned so clearly to idolatry that God permitted the Northern Kingdom of Israel to be carried into captivity by the Assyrians in 722-721 B.C.

By 606 B.C., the Southern Kingdom of Judah was ready for similar punishment from God. King Nebuchadnezzar of Babylon did not conquer the Kingdom of Judah in a single campaign; he did so in three campaigns, ending in 586 B.C. This great Babylonian monarch inaugurated what our Lord called the "times of the Gentiles" (Luke 21:24). This phrase is the political designation for the rule of the Gentiles over God's chosen people, Israel. This lengthy period has not yet ended.

In the first chapter of Daniel, the Lord reveals that when the Babylonian invaders entered Jerusalem, they looted the important sacred vessels of the house of God. The Kingdom of Judah had begun its final decline under the reign of Jehoiakim (2 Kings 24:2). The loss of power continued during the three-month reign of Jehoiachin (2 Kings 24:8-16) and was completed under the reign of Zedekiah, who was taken captive in 586 B.C. and died a prisoner in Babylon (2 Kings 24:17—25:21).

1 The Preparation of God's Servant

In the third year of the reign of Jehoiakim king of Judah, Nebuchadnezzar king of Babylon came to Jerusalem and besieged it. ² And the Lord gave Jehoiakim king of Judah into his hand, along with some of the vessels of the house of God; and he brought them to the land of Shinar, to the house of his god, and he brought the vessels into the treasury of his god. ³ Then the king ordered Ashpenaz, the chief of his officials, to bring in some of the sons of Israel, including some of the royal family and of the nobles, ⁴ youths in whom was no defect, who were good-looking, showing intelligence in every branch of wisdom, endowed with understanding, and discerning knowledge, and who had ability for serving in the king's court; and he ordered him to teach them the literature and language of the Chaldeans. ⁵ And the king appointed for them a daily ration from the king's choice food and from the wine which he drank, and appointed that they should be educated three years, at the end of which they were to enter the king's personal service. ⁶ Now among them from the sons of Judah were Daniel, Hananiah, Mishael and Azariah. ⁷ Then the commander of the officials assigned new names to them; and to Daniel he assigned the name Belteshazzar, to Hananiah Shadrach, to Mishael Meshach, and to Azariah Abed-nego.

⁸ But Daniel made up his mind that he would not defile himself with the king's choice food or with the wine which he drank; so he sought permission from the commander of the officials that he might not defile himself. ⁹ Now God granted Daniel favor and compassion in the sight of the commander of the officials, ¹⁰ and the commander of the officials said to Daniel, "I am afraid of my lord the king, who has appointed your food and your drink; for

why should he see your faces looking more haggard than the youths who are your own age? Then you would make me forfeit my head to the king." [11] But Daniel said to the overseer whom the commander of the officials had appointed over Daniel, Hananiah, Mishael and Azariah, [12] "Please test your servants for ten days, and let us be given some vegetables to eat and water to drink. [13] Then let our appearance be observed in your presence, and the appearance of the youths who are eating the king's choice food; and deal with your servants according to what you see."

[14] So he listened to them in this matter and tested them for ten days. [15] And at the end of ten days their appearance seemed better and they were fatter than all the youths who had been eating the king's choice food. [16] So the overseer continued to withhold their choice food and the wine they were to drink, and kept giving them vegetables.

[17] And as for these four youths, God gave them knowledge and intelligence in every branch of literature and wisdom; Daniel even understood all kinds of visions and dreams. [18] Then at the end of the days which the king had specified for presenting them, the commander of the officials presented them before Nebuchadnezzar. [19] And the king talked with them, and out of them all not one was found like Daniel, Hananiah, Mishael and Azariah; so they entered the king's personal service. [20] And as for every matter of wisdom and understanding about which the king consulted them, he found them ten times better than all the magicians and conjurers who were in all his realm. [21] And Daniel continued until the first year of Cyrus the king.

Verse 1: This recounts the invasion of Jerusalem by the king of Babylon. Jehoiakim had already died in disgrace (Jer. 22:17-19), before the invader ever arrived.

Verse 2: It was the Lord who gave Jehoiakim into the hand of the king of Babylon. Nebuchadnezzar took sacred vessels from the house of God on several occasions, carrying them off to the temple of the Babylonian god, Bel-Merodach.

Verse 3: Nebuchadnezzar ordered that the finest young men of Judah be brought before him. Josephus, a Jewish historian of the first century A.D., claims the young men were all related to Zedekiah. His claim seems likely in view of this passage. Daniel was included in the first deportation to Babylon, for Nebuchadnezzar seems to have desired valuable additions to his empire rather than mere masses of prisoners. The men chosen were all quite young, in order to obtain the greatest benefit from training them.

Verse 4: These young men are spoken of as being "youths"; Daniel's age at this time has been estimated at about nineteen. They were to learn Babylonian science, which was full of theological, astrological, and magical elements. Nebuchadnezzar was training these young men to become his "brain trust."

Verse 5: It was customary for a king to feed his guests with food from his own table, so the young men of Israel were to be served in this fashion during their training, which was to last three years. The king discerned these youths' ability and so arranged not only the subject of their studies, but their duration as well. Afterward, they were to enter into the king's personal service, advising and administering in his palace.

Verse 6: Four of the captives from Judah were singled out, although surely there were others in the program. Each of their names was an eloquent testimony to the power and grace of God. The name Daniel means "God is my judge"; Hananiah means "The LORD is gracious"; Mishael means "Who is what God is?" or "Who is comparable to God?"; and Azariah means "LORD is my help" or "Whom the LORD helps." Each name had either "God" or "the LORD" in it.

Verse 7: These four Israelites were given new Babylonian names to signify their new standing in the Babylonian Empire — and also to help them forget their former country and faith. It seems the world always tries to blot out the distinctive marks of a believer; you see, the new names gave testimony not to the God of Israel, but to the gods of the

Babylonians. The name Belteshazzar speaks of the prince of Bel; Shadrach means "Inspired (or illumined) by the sun-god"; Meshach means "Who is like Shach (Venus)?"; and Abed-nego means "Servant of the shining fire." So instead of being named in dedication to the Lord, these four youths were renamed in dedication to the gods of the Babylonians.

Verse 8: Daniel resolved in his own mind that he would not defile himself by eating food that was forbidden by the Law of Moses, and he was joined in this by the other three youths. In those days it was customary to throw a small portion of the meat and wine from each meal onto the hearth, thus consecrating the entire meal as an offering to the gods. To take part in such a feast would have been to sanction idolatry (cf. 1 Cor. 8), even after the distinction between clean and unclean meat had been discarded, as in the New Testament.

Like Moses, Daniel was unwilling to enjoy the pleasures of sin, even for a season. But although he had resolved in his heart not to defile himself, he realized that he was still under the king's authority. So, in order to do all things decently and in order, he asked permission to be exempted from eating the food prescribed for his class.

This was a great moral and spiritual decision for Daniel. He had witnessed the great upheavals in Israel during the declining years of the monarchy, and the transition from Israel's independence to the "times of the Gentiles" was certainly not lost on him. Yet he was mature enough to recognize the spiritual significance of these events. He determined, therefore, to walk in the way of faith and in obedience to God's will. He would not drift with the currents of the times, come what may. His actions were a combination of godliness, courtesy, and courage.

Daniel and his friends were faithful by remaining separated from the world. When we remain separated from the world, we are prepared to receive God's communication through the Scriptures. In too many cases, prophetic study is undertaken by very unspiritual people. If we are to gain the most from the study of this book, we must bear in mind that the visions and truths in this book were revealed to a spiritually minded man who was separated from the sin and degradation of his day.

It would have been so easy for Daniel to shift responsibility in this matter from himself to the king. He could have claimed that while he was under Nebuchadnezzar's authority he *had* to obey. Had not God permitted them to be taken captive to Babylon? But these Hebrew youths looked beyond earthly issues and saw in the king's order a test of faith. Would they remain true to God, even in idolatrous Babylon? Here was a remarkable opportunity to serve God in a strange place, where so little was known of God.

Verse 9: God caused Daniel to be regarded with favor by the commander of the Babylonian officials, and he was treated with compassion. It is interesting how God causes the godly and faithful to find favor in the eyes of others, such as Joseph did in the eyes of Pharaoh. No man has ever lost out by being faithful to the Lord and His will.

Verse 10: The commander of the officials was concerned, and rightly so. He was personally responsible to the king for the well-being of these young men; and should any ill effects result from altering their diet, Nebuchadnezzar could have him beheaded.

Verse 11: When Daniel's appeal to the commander failed, he then spoke to the overseer who had been appointed over them.

Verse 12: Daniel asked to be allowed to eat vegetables and drink water for ten days, as a test of their petition. They sought to be temperate in all things, body and soul.

Verse 13: Daniel was willing to be put to the test and to suffer the consequences; the Lord has more than one way of sustaining His own. It may seem that this places undue stress on trivial matters, but we must be aware that the only way to progress in one's relationship with God is to be faithful in the little things at hand. The need for holiness in every area of our lives cannot be overemphasized. One who seeks to glorify the Lord in what the world calls trivial details will be sensitive to magnify God in greater things. **Verses 14 and 15:** The overseer of the Hebrews agreed to this trial period of ten days, and thus they began their new diet. At the end of the prescribed ten days of testing, Daniel and his friends were found to be looking healthier and of better complexion than all the other youths dining at the king's table.

There has been some discussion about whether this result was natural or miraculous. We recognize that temperance does result in better health and greater energy, yet this entire account leads us to believe that in this instance, God caused Daniel's godly position to result in blessing even beyond what could normally have been expected. Performing the will of God is like marrow to the bones, and performing one's own will can be like rottenness to the bones. **Verse 16:** Once they had passed the test, the overseer no longer feared to allow them to continue in the manner they had chosen. This was doubtless a visible testimony to the pagan, who had seen evidence of the blessing of God in their lives.

Verse 17: You can be sure that Daniel and his companions applied themselves to the task at hand and showed diligence throughout. But beyond that, the hand of God was upon them to enlighten their minds and quicken their native faculties for His use. In Daniel's case, the Lord also gave him special understanding of dreams and visions. He was not dependent, as the Babylonian magicians were, on mere human wisdom, but the Lord imparted to him what could never be naturally understood. He was imbued with a prophetic spirit, which gave men supernatural insight into the will and plan of God.

Verses 18 to 20: Their examination day finally arrived. The four young men had to stand before the king for his scrutiny, as did the others. Would separation to God make a difference? The result would now be seen. When King Nebuchadnezzar tested his "brain trust," it was found that Daniel and his companions were far superior to all the rest. Notice that because the king was a man of ability and wisdom, he arrived at his conclusions by testing them personally. He discovered that they were not just a little better than the rest, but ten times better. The four were then chosen for responsible positions of service to the king.

Verse 21: Chapter 1, which admittedly is an introduction to the whole prophecy, closes with the remark that Daniel lived until the first year of the reign of Cyrus, about 536 B.C. This does not mean that Daniel did not live beyond that date, for Daniel 10:1 reveals that he lived until the third year of the reign of Cyrus. This statement is intended to show that God permitted His faithful servant to live until the end of the Babylonian Captivity. It was Cyrus (Ezra 1:1-3) who permitted the captives to return to Jerusalem and to rebuild the temple as of old.

To that hour, God graciously sustained His servant: having believed God for the deliverance when he could not see it, he was rewarded by being allowed to see the delivered remnant enter into the fulfillment of the promise of God.

2 The Vision of the Image

Now in the second year of the reign of Nebuchadnezzar, Nebuchadnezzar had dreams; and his spirit was troubled and his sleep left him. ² Then the king gave orders to call in the magicians, the conjurers, the sorcerers and the Chaldeans, to tell the king his dreams. So they came in and stood before the king. ³ And the king said to them, "I had a dream, and my spirit is anxious to understand the dream."

⁴ Then the Chaldeans spoke to the king in Aramaic: "O king, live forever! Tell the dream to your servants, and we will declare the interpretation." ⁵ The king answered and said to the Chaldeans, "The command from me is firm: if you do not make known to me the dream and its interpretation, you will be torn limb from limb, and your houses will be made a rubbish heap. ⁶ But if you declare the dream and its interpretation, you will receive from me gifts and a reward and great honor; therefore declare to me the dream and its interpretation." ⁷ They answered a second time and said, "Let the king tell the dream to his servants, and we will declare the interpretation." ⁸ The king answered and said, "I know for certain that you are bargaining for time, inasmuch as you have seen that the command from me is firm, ⁹ that if you do not make the dream known to me, there is only one decree for you. For you have agreed together to speak lying and corrupt words before me until the situation is changed; therefore tell me the dream, that I may know that you can declare to me its interpretation." ¹⁰ The Chaldeans answered the king and said, "There is not a man on earth who could declare the matter for the king, inasmuch as no great king or ruler has *ever* asked anything like this of any magician, conjurer or Chaldean. ¹¹ Moreover, the thing which the king demands is difficult, and there is no one else who could declare it to

the king except gods, whose dwelling place is not with *mortal*
flesh." ¹²Because of this the king became indignant and very
furious, and gave orders to destroy all the wise men of Babylon.
¹³ So the decree went forth that the wise men should be slain; and
they looked for Daniel and his friends to kill *them*.

¹⁴ Then Daniel replied with discretion and discernment to
Arioch, the captain of the king's bodyguard, who had gone forth to
slay the wise men of Babylon; ¹⁵ he answered and said to Arioch,
the king's commander. "For what reason is the decree from the
king *so* urgent?" Then Arioch informed Daniel about the matter.
¹⁶ So Daniel went in and requested of the king that he would give
him time, in order that he might declare the interpretation to the
king.

¹⁷ Then Daniel went to his house and informed his friends,
Hananiah, Mishael and Azariah, about the matter, ¹⁸ in order that
they might request compassion from the God of heaven concerning this mystery, so that Daniel and his friends might not be
destroyed with the rest of the wise men of Babylon. ¹⁹ Then the
mystery was revealed to Daniel in a night vision. Then Daniel
blessed the God of heaven;

²⁰ Daniel answered and said,

"Let the name of God be blessed forever and ever,
For wisdom and power belong to Him.

²¹ And it is He who changes the times and the epochs;
He removes kings and establishes kings;
He gives wisdom to wise men,
And knowledge to men of understanding.

²² It is He who reveals the profound and hidden things;
He knows what is in the darkness,
And the light dwells with Him.
To Thee, O God of my fathers, I give thanks and praise,
For Thou hast given me wisdom and power;
Even now Thou hast made known to me what we requested
of Thee,
For Thou hast made known to us the king's matter."

²⁴ Therefore, Daniel went in to Arioch, whom the king had
appointed to destroy the wise men of Babylon; he went and spoke
to him as follows: "Do not destroy the wise men of Babylon! Take

me into the king's presence, and I will declare the interpretation to the king."

²⁵ Then Arioch hurriedly brought Daniel into the king's presence and spoke to him as follows: "I have found a man among the exiles from Judah who can make the interpretation known to the king!" ²⁶ The king answered and said to Daniel, whose name was Belteshazzar, "Are you able to make known to me the dream which I have seen and its interpretation?" ²⁷ Daniel answered before the king and said, "As for the mystery about which the king has inquired, neither wise men, conjurers, magicians *nor* diviners are able to declare *it* to the king. ²⁸ However, there is a God in heaven who reveals mysteries, and He has made known to King Nebuchadnezzar what will take place in the latter days. This was your dream and the visions in your mind *while* on your bed. ²⁹ As for you, O king, *while* on your bed your thoughts turned to what would take place in the future; and He who reveals mysteries has made known to you what will take place. ³⁰ But as for me, this mystery has not been revealed to me for any wisdom residing in me more than *in* any *other* living man, but for the purpose of making the interpretation known to the king, and that you may understand the thoughts of your mind.

³¹ "You, O king, were looking and behold, there was a single great statue; that statue, which was large and of extraordinary splendor, was standing in front of you, and its appearance was awesome. ³² The head of that statue *was made* of fine gold, its breast and its arms of silver, its belly and its thighs of bronze, ³³ its legs of iron, its feet partly of iron and partly of clay. ³⁴ You continued looking until a stone was cut out without hands, and it struck the statue on its feet of iron and clay, and crushed them. ³⁵ Then the iron, the clay, the bronze, the silver and the gold were crushed all at the same time, and became like chaff from the summer threshing floors; and the wind carried them away so that not a trace of them was found. But the stone that struck the statue became a great mountain and filled the whole earth.

³⁶ "This *was* the dream; now we shall tell its interpretation before the king. ³⁷ You, O king, are the king of kings, to whom the God of heaven has given the kingdom, the power, the strength, and the glory; ³⁸ and wherever the sons of men dwell, *or* the beasts

of the field, or the birds of the sky, He has given *them* into your hand and has caused you to rule over them all. You are the head of gold. [39] And after you there will arise another kingdom inferior to you, then another third kingdom of bronze, which will rule over all the earth. [40] Then there will be a fourth kingdom as strong as iron; inasmuch as iron crushes and shatters all things, so, like iron that breaks in pieces, it will crush and break all these in pieces. [41] And in that you saw the feet and toes, partly of potter's clay and partly of iron, it will be a divided kingdom; but it will have in it the toughness of iron, inasmuch as you saw the iron mixed with common clay. [42] And *as* the toes of the feet *were* partly of iron and partly of pottery, so some of the kingdom will be strong and part of it will be brittle. [43] And in that you saw the iron mixed with common clay, they will combine with one another in the seed of men; but they will not adhere to one another, even as iron does not combine with pottery. [44] And in the days of those kings the God of heaven will set up a kingdom which will never be destroyed, and *that* kingdom will not be left for another people; it will crush and put an end to all these kingdoms, but it will itself endure forever. [45] Inasmuch as you saw that a stone was cut out of the mountain without hands and that it crushed the iron, the bronze, the clay, the silver, and the gold, the great God has made known to the king what will take place in the future; so the dream is true, and its interpretation is trustworthy."

[46] Then King Nebuchadnezzar fell on his face and did homage to Daniel, and gave orders to present to him an offering and fragrant incense. [47] The king answered Daniel and said, "Surely your God is a God of gods and a Lord of kings and a revealer of mysteries, since you have been able to reveal this mystery." [48] Then the king promoted Daniel and gave him many great gifts, and he made him ruler over the whole province of Babylon and chief prefect over all the wise men of Babylon. [49] And Daniel made request of the king, and he appointed Shadrach, Meshach and Abed-nego over the administration of the province of Babylon, while Daniel *was* at the king's court.

Introduction

The second chapter of Daniel has been justly called "the alphabet of prophecy." Whoever wishes to understand the prophetic Scriptures must come to this chapter for the broad outline of God's future program for the nations, for Israel, and for the glorious kingdom of Messiah. This outline is the simple but comprehensive framework of a multitude of future events. No political document can compare with it, and its importance cannot be overstated.

It may seem strange that this revelation is given in the form of a dream, and that to a pagan king. However, because he was a pagan, Nebuchadnezzar did not have the Scriptures at hand. The Lord thus reached into the king's innermost consciousness in his sleep and imparted His message in the manner described in Job 33:13-18.

In those days, Nebuchadnezzar was ruler of most of the civilized world—and much of the barbarian world as well. Although he did not exercise total authority over the entire region, Nebuchadnezzar had been given by God the right to all the nations. Rule had been granted to this Gentile king because God had set aside the earthly rule of Israel after many years of backsliding and disobedience. As we have seen, this change marks the beginning of the "times of the Gentiles" spoken of by our Lord in Luke 21:24.

Verse 1: When Nebuchadnezzar had first invaded Judah, he was not yet king but ruled as a subordinate of his father, King Nabopolassar. As this chapter opens, Nebuchadnezzar had been sole, absolute ruler for two years.

Notice that this verse refers to dreams in the plural, because the dream consisted of several parts. As the most powerful man of his day, the king had doubtless given much thought to the course of his rule and had probably wondered more than once what the destiny of his realm would be. Thoughtful men and women know they cannot remain on earth forever, so they are concerned about what the future holds.

It is important to notice that it was not to Daniel but to Nebuchadnezzar that God disclosed the doom of the first kingdom and all those to follow, until the kingdom of the Lord is realized on earth. Remember, God communicated to Nebuchadnezzar in dreams because the king was a heathen and did not have access to the Scriptures of the Jews. But unlike the Pharaoh of Egypt, who remembered his dream (Gen. 41:1-8), Nebuchadnezzar forgot his, probably out of fright. The heathen frequently attach great importance to dreams.

Verse 2: Having forgotten the dream and being concerned for its meaning, the king naturally turned to his learned advisors, magicians and astrologers who muttered and whispered their incantations, sorcerers, and probably priests of Bel-marduk, who were known as Chaldeans.

Verse 3: The king was frank to admit that he had forgotten his dream. Some have questioned whether Nebuchadnezzar really forgot; perhaps this was just the king's way of testing his men. It seems more plausible, though, that he really forgot it, because of the strange character of the dream. The details were blacked out from his memory; and if he had a foreboding of disaster, it could have formed the basis for the dream whereby God outlined the course of the centuries to come.

Verse 4: In the original text, the language changes at this point from Hebrew to Aramaic, and appropriately so. The content of this dream concerns the Gentile world, so the medium of revelation to the Gentiles is a Gentile language. When the prophecies concern the Jews in Jerusalem, the Hebrew language is employed. In the original text, this Aramaic passage continues through Daniel 7:28.

Charlatans that these Chaldean advisors were, they asked to be told the king's dream so that they could manipulate it for their own purposes.

Verse 5: When men affect to supernatural knowledge they do not possess, they are apt to bring on their own punishment. In this case, the king's answer was immediate: if these advisors failed to make known to the king the dream and its interpretation, they would be cut to pieces. If there is any doubt that Nebuchadnezzar would carry out such a threat, we need only recall the punishment he had poured out upon Zedekiah, the wicked king of Judah: he slew Zedekiah's sons before his eyes, slew all the princes of Judah, blinded Zedekiah, and then deported him in chains to Babylon, where he died in prison (Jer. 52:1-11).

Verse 6: The other half of the king's reply was a promise. If they could declare to him the dream and its interpretation, he would shower them with lavish gifts and honors as their reward.

Verse 7: According to the traditions of Babylonian sorcery, it was reasonable for the king to tell them the content of his dream. In this case, however, they were asking for something he could not give. By this time the king must have doubted their candor.

Verse 8: Nebuchadnezzar realized they were stalling for time and that they hoped to postpone the matter until the king was in a better mood.

Verse 9: The king displayed common sense when he told his advisors that he would have the best assurance of the accuracy of their interpretation if only they could recount to him the substance of his dream. He accused them of conspiring to answer him deceitfully to win a delay. In the ancient Near East, much was made of lucky and unlucky days. Sadly, our own culture seems to be increasingly caught up in such occult beliefs.

Verse 10: Now, God caused these heathens to declare their helplessness with their own mouths. He would show, by contrast, how He can reveal His secrets through His servants, even though they are but mortal men.

The king's advisors argued that they should never have

been asked to fulfill this request in the first place. Because such a thing had never been done before, they argued that it could not be done now.

Verse 11: The magicians appealed to the gods of the Babylonians, who were supposed to be able to help them in such situations. Unfortunately, such gods are unable to communicate with mortal men, or to help them in their time of need, because they are not God at all. Since these gods could not help them, the king's advisors argued that the task was beyond the abilities of mortal men, and they should not be expected to perform it.

Verse 12: In his indignation, Nebuchadnezzar ordered the destruction of all the wise men of Babylon. Although Daniel and his companions do not seem to have been present before the king, the decree was so general that it would have to include them as well.

Verse 13: We will learn later that when Daniel finally intervenes in this situation, the executions had not yet been carried out. God so arranged it that the inadequacy of human wisdom was demonstrated before His power could be revealed through His servant.

Verse 14: Daniel first contacted the man who was entrusted to carry out the royal decree of execution.

Verse 15: Daniel's question definitely implies that the matter was by no means concluded; the king's request was not as impossible as his wise men had made it out to be.

Verse 16: Evidently Daniel was unaware of the situation until this time, for he asked the king to grant him time and assured him that there would be an interpretation forthcoming. Although the king would not give his advisors more time, he granted Daniel's request. The reason for this is that the king was already convinced of the Chaldeans' duplicity, because they had sought the substance of the dream before they would interpret it. Daniel had made no such stipulation in his petition; the God who would supply the interpretation would also supply the content of the dream.

Verse 17: One reason Daniel sought more time from the king was that he wanted to enlist the prayer support of his godly companions. Daniel had learned the important spiritual lesson that there is great power in the united prayer of believers.

Verse 18: The four young men prayed to the God of heaven for compassion, that through His intervention they might be spared from the decreed executions. The fact that they called on "the God of heaven" is full of meaning. Every careful student of the Bible knows that the names of God are used purposefully in Scripture. When God is described in relation to the Gentiles or to creation, He is known as "Elohim." When a passage emphasizes the redeeming God or the covenant-keeping God, He is known as "Jehovah" or "the LORD." The name "the God of heaven" appears prominently in passages that relate to the captivity and scattering of Israel, such as in Ezra, Nehemiah, and Daniel.

When God's people are enslaved on earth, His glory is not revealed on earth as it should be. He is disowned on earth and referred to as the "God of heaven." However, when His Son, the Lord Jesus Christ, comes to reign on earth, God will once again be acclaimed the Lord of all the earth.

Verse 19: There are three important characteristics of this prayer that should be noted: exaltation of God, divine intervention, and worshipful praise.

Verse 20: This prayer by Daniel is full of scriptural language; he extols the acts of God's wisdom and might.

Verse 21: Here Daniel gently hints that the king's dream deals with the succession of kings and kingdoms. The histories of empires are not a matter of accident, as the heathen thought, but are determined by God. Power and rule are His to delegate: He can—and does—remove kings (Rom. 13:1).

Verse 22: Only God can reveal that which man cannot discern for himself. The deep and secret things of the spiritual realm are solely in the power of God to disclose. No darkness can hide from Him, for He is the source, not only of physical light, but also of all spiritual enlightenment and illumination (1 Cor. 2:10-14; 1 John 1:5).

Verse 23: Daniel demonstrated true humility, as he took no credit for the wisdom and power he had been given; instead, he gave God all the glory. Daniel had prayed for specific ends, and God answered him in a specific way.

Verse 24: Once the dream and its interpretation had been revealed to Daniel, he asked to be admitted into the presence of the king. He dared not delay; lives were at stake. He had to give the king the answer to what was troubling him.

Verse 25: Human nature being what it is, Arioch claimed credit for finding an interpreter of the dream, even though he had not sought Daniel out.

Verse 26: Because all the wise men and experienced counselors of state had been unable to answer the king, he expressed surprise that a man as young as Daniel should be able to meet the challenge.

Verse 27: In answer, Daniel replied in all honesty and humility that he could not take credit for having discerned the dream and its interpretation. The king's wise men had been correct: no mere mortal could have fulfilled Nebuchadnezzar's charge. The solution to the problem, the power of prediction, lay with the God of heaven and not with the useless gods of Babylon.

Verse 28: In the dream, God's intention was to disclose to the king the events that would transpire in the latter days. The expression "latter days" is very important in Scripture and refers to the future in general, and in particular to the days of the Messiah in the final period of human history, before the eternal state.

Verse 29: All the centuries of the future were to be revealed to the king. No dream, before this or since, has ever revealed so much of world history. It covered the entire period from Nebuchadnezzar's own day to the end of time on earth.

Verse 30: We might forgive Daniel if he had taken a little credit for making known the dream and its interpretation, since it was such a great revelation. However, this man of God disclaimed any merit in himself. Rather, God gave the dream for the king's enlightenment, and surely He intended for the king to profit by the warning it contained. Because man has no resources of himself in these matters, human pride is completely out of the picture. In this account, then, the wisdom of this world was first shown to be bankrupt, and then God gloriously intervened.

Verse 31: In his dream, King Nebuchadnezzar saw a single, great statue. Have you ever wondered why the dream was given to the king in the form of a colossal statue? The symbols used in the Bible are carefully chosen, and they cannot be interchanged without doing violence to the intent of both the human writer and the Holy Spirit who inspired him.

The figure of a man was employed here because God wished to make known what would transpire during man's day, the ages in which mortal man ruled the earth. Here, in one panoramic sweep, the whole history of human civilization is spread before us, from the days of Nebuchadnezzar to the end of time.

Verses 32 through 35: Daniel next described the great image the king had seen in his dream. The great statue was in the form of a man, whose head was made of gold. Its arms and chest were made of silver, and its belly and thighs of bronze. Its legs were made of iron, and its feet of both iron and clay.

Daniel went on to recount that the king saw a stone cut out without hands, and that stone struck the statue on its feet and destroyed it. The stone then grew to become a great mountain and to fill the whole world.

Upon hearing this, the king immediately remembered the dream.

Verse 36: Daniel went on to tell the interpretation of the dream.

Verses 37 and 38: Nebuchadnezzar himself, king of the Babylonian Empire, was the head of gold in this dream. The gold and riches of Babylon were well known in the ancient world (Isa. 45:1-3). It should be noticed that Nebuchadnezzar derived his authority from God and was ultimately responsible to Him. His rule was intended to be as far-reaching and complete as possible.

Verse 39: Another kingdom would arise after the fall of the Babylonian Empire, which was to end with the grandson of Nebuchadnezzar. This new kingdom, symbolized by the silver arms and chest, is identified with the Medo-Persian Empire, according to 5:28 and 8:20.

Was this second empire really inferior to the first? Indeed it was, for whereas Nebuchadnezzar ruled as an absolute monarch, in the Medo-Persian Empire the power of the central government was limited by the increasing strength of the nobility, and by the growing independence of the provinces. Nebuchadnezzar's word was law and was unquestioned; Darius the Mede, by contrast, was repeatedly frustrated by the demands of the nobles (see, for example, chap. 6).

A third kingdom, symbolized by the statue's bronze belly and thighs, is identified with the Macedonian Empire of Alexander the Great. This Greek empire conquered the Persians and at its height ruled the entire civilized world.

Verse 40: A fourth and last kingdom is symbolized by the statue's legs of iron and feet of iron and clay. This kingdom is identified with the Roman Empire, which was in power at the time of the incarnation of our Lord Jesus Christ.

Verses 41 through 43: In this symbol of the Roman

Empire, the feet of the great statue are a mixture of iron and clay. These two extremes indicate that Rome would be characterized by both strength and weakness. Historically, Rome was a combination of both a democratic government (during the Roman Republic) and an imperial government (during the Roman Empire). In the king's dream, when the stone struck the statue's feet, the whole statue was shattered. Empires, which seem so permanent to men, will not be able to stand when the Lord visits His wrath upon them.

Following the resurrection and ascension of the Lord, the Roman Empire survived intact for another five centuries, after which it split into the Western Roman and the Eastern Roman (Byzantine) empires. The Western empire was conquered in A.D. 476, and the Eastern empire survived another thousand years, until it was conquered by the Turks in 1453.

It is remarkable to consider how faithfully the course of world history has followed this predicted outline in the book of Daniel. As he had been informed, Nebuchadnezzar inaugurated the "times of the Gentiles" during his reign, which lasted from 606 to 536 B.C. The Medo-Persian Empire, which followed, continued these times from 536 B.C. until it was conquered by the Macedonian Empire of Alexander the Great in 330 B.C. Finally, in 65 B.C., the Roman army wrested control of Judea from Alexander's successors, and the prophecy of the four kingdoms was fulfilled.

Notice that at the time Daniel explained this prophecy, only the first of these four kingdoms had arrived on the world stage; the other three empires did not yet exist. Daniel could never have guessed his way so successfully down the centuries of history. The Lord alone knows the course of the days to come, and, as He revealed in this prophecy, the story of human history is not one of progress but of gradual degeneration.

As we study this fourth kingdom, we must not overlook the fact that it appears in two different forms in the book of

Daniel. In this passage, it is described in its two-stage form, whereas in the seventh chapter of Daniel it is described in its tenfold form. This tenfold arrangement of the Roman Empire has never been witnessed on earth, even to this day. That can only mean that the Roman Empire, long dormant, has not yet completed its prescribed role in world affairs.

As we shall see when we study chapter 7, the ten toes of the statue represent ten kings, who will simultaneously rule over a confederated empire in the land that formerly made up the old Roman Empire. This arrangement is so different from the form of the ancient Roman Empire that we cannot believe it refers to that.

Verse 44: If this interpretation is correct, what historical event would correspond to the falling of the stone on the statue, smashing it? The stone that fell from heaven cannot be understood as the birth of Christ into the world, nor as the peaceful spread of the gospel. The birth of Jesus was not a catastrophe that shattered all the empires of the world; on the contrary, the Roman authorities joined with Jewish religious leaders in putting Christ to death. Similarly, the peaceful spread of the gospel has not destroyed all world empires, either. We do not know, nor are we authorized to say, just when the final cataclysm will strike.

The "stone made without hands" is of more than passing interest. Psalm 118:22 predicts, "The stone which the build-ers rejected has become the chief corner stone." According to the New Testament, this refers to Christ (Matt. 21:42-44; Acts 4:10-12; Eph. 2:19-21). The Jewish religious leaders did not understand the work of this "stone" and rejected Him. But rejected though He was by men (Isa. 53:3), He was eminently approved by God to sit at His right hand in glory (Psalm 110:1).

However, not all those in Israel were blind to the glory of the Son of God; Isaiah 28:16 speaks of the remnant who find in Christ a tried and precious cornerstone, a solid foundation. Similarly, Zechariah 3:9 describes that stone as having been engraved with inscriptions that are conducive to the life and blessing of all who receive it.

Verse 45: The primary concern of this passage is the question, How are the nations of the world related to this "stone"? The clear testimony of Scripture is that unbelieving nations will continue to reject the grace of God in Jesus Christ until the day of judgment arrives, from which there is no escape (Matt. 22:1-13).

Global empires will be crushed by Christ and ground to powder. They shall be broken and driven away, just as chaff is driven from the threshing floor. In the ancient Near East, it was customary to winnow wheat in a high place. When the wheat was then thrown into the air, the chaff was carried away in the wind, while the wheat returned to earth to be gathered into the barn.

When will this stone fall and smash the great statue? No one can say for certain, but it must follow catastrophe and the formation of a ten-kingdom federation on the territory of the old Roman Empire. It will have a supreme head, a political leader of great power. He will not be able to bring peace to the world but will be crushed by the returning Lord Jesus Christ, who then will establish peace on earth.

Although some may deny that a revival of the Roman Empire is possible, it is evident that European thought is moving more and more along these lines to counter the growing strength of that northern colossus, Communist Russia. In fact, the balance of power will be difficult to preserve unless the "beast of the north" is counterbalanced. How soon that coalition will be formed is impossible to say. But before these events come to fruition, the church will be caught away into heaven, just as the Lord promised (John 14:1-3; 1 Thess. 4:13-18). All believers in the Lord Jesus Christ will be taken to be with Him before these final events are fulfilled on earth.

Verse: 46: The king was overwhelmed by the wisdom the Lord had given to Daniel. Here, in one dream's interpretation, was the history of world empires from Nebuchadnezzar's own reign to the coming reign of the Lord Jesus Christ.

Verse 47: In chapters to come, we shall see that Nebuchadnezzar did not learn as much as he might have from this dream. Although he admitted the incomparable wisdom of the Lord, this experience failed to convict him of his personal need for God.

Verse 48: Nebuchadnezzar rewarded Daniel for making known to him his dream and its interpretation, giving him gifts and authority over the province of Babylon.

Verse 49: Daniel's generous heart is shown in the fact that he sought to share his reward with his three companions in prayer. This chapter ends on a prophetic note: Daniel, the slave of men and servant of God, received the homage of a prostrate king just as the Lord Jesus Christ, who was submissive to men and the servant of God, will receive the homage of all men. "At the name of Jesus every knee should bow, of those who are in heaven, and on earth, and under the earth, and...every tongue should confess that Jesus Christ is Lord, to the glory of God the Father" (Phil. 2:10-11).

3 The Golden Image of Nebuchadnezzar

NEBUCHADNEZZAR the king made an image of gold, the height of which *was* sixty cubits *and* its width six cubits; he set it up on the plain of Dura in the province of Babylon. ² Then Nebuchadnezzar the king sent *word* to assemble the satraps, the prefects and the governors, the counselors, the treasurers, the judges, the magistrates and all the rulers of the provinces to come to the dedication of the image that Nebuchadnezzar the king had set up. ³ Then the satraps, the prefects and the governors, the counselors, the treasurers, the judges, the magistrates and all the rulers of the provinces were assembled for the dedication of the image that Nebuchadnezzar the king had set up; and they stood before the image that Nebuchadnezzar had set up. ⁴ Then the herald loudly proclaimed: "To you the command is given, O peoples, nations and *men of every* language, ⁵ that at the moment you hear the sound of the horn, flute, lyre, trigon, psaltery, bagpipe, and all kinds of music, you are to fall down and worship the golden image that Nebuchadnezzar the king has set up. ⁶ But whoever does not fall down and worship shall immediately be cast into the midst of a furnace of blazing fire." ⁷ Therefore at that time, when all the peoples heard the sound of the horn, flute, lyre, trigon, psaltery, bagpipe, and all kinds of music, all the peoples, nations and *men of every* language fell down *and* worshiped the golden image that Nebuchadnezzar the king had set up.

⁸ For this reason at that time certain Chaldeans came forward and brought charges against the Jews. ⁹ They responded and said to Nebuchadnezzar the king: "O king, live forever! ¹⁰ You yourself, O king, have made a decree that every man who hears the sound of the horn, flute, lyre, trigon, psaltery, and bagpipe, and all kinds of music,

is to fall down and worship the golden image. [11] But whoever does not fall down and worship shall be cast into the midst of a furnace of blazing fire. [12] There are certain Jews whom you have appointed over the administration of the province of Babylon, *namely* Shadrach, Meshach, and Abed-nego. These men, O king, have disregarded you; they do not serve your gods or worship the golden image which you have set up."

[13] Then Nebuchadnezzar in rage and anger gave orders to bring Shadrach, Meshach, and Abed-nego; then these men were brought before the king. [14] Nebuchadnezzar responded and said to them, "Is it true, Shadrach, Meshach and Abed-nego, that you do not serve my gods or worship the golden image that I have set up? [15] Now if you are ready, at the moment you hear the sound of the horn, flute, lyre, trigon, psaltery, and bagpipe, and all kinds of music, to fall down and worship the image that I have made, *very well.* But if you will not worship, you will immediately be cast into the midst of a furnace of blazing fire; and what god is there who can deliver you out of my hands?" [16] Shadrach, Meshach and Abed-nego answered and said to the king, "O Nebuchadnezzar, we do not need to give you an answer concerning this. [17] If it be *so,* our God whom we serve is able to deliver us from the furnace of blazing fire; and He will deliver us out of your hand, O king. [18] But *even* if *He does* not, let it be known to you, O king, that we are not going to serve your gods or worship the golden image that you have set up."

[19] Then Nebuchadnezzar was filled with wrath, and his facial expression was altered toward Shadrach, Meshach and Abed-nego. He answered by giving orders to heat the furnace seven times more than it was usually heated. [20] And he commanded certain valiant warriors who *were* in his army to tie up Shadrach, Meshach and Abed-nego, in order to cast *them* into the furnace of blazing fire. [21] Then these men were tied up in their trousers, their coats, their caps and their *other* clothes, and were cast into the midst of the furnace of blazing fire. [22] For this reason, because the king's command *was* urgent and the furnace had been made extremely hot, the flame of the fire slew those men who carried up Shadrach, Meshach and Abed-nego. [23] But these three men, Shadrach, Meshach and Abed-nego, fell into the midst of the furnace of blazing fire *still* tied up.

[24] Then Nebuchadnezzar the king was astounded and stood up in

haste; he responded and said to his high officials, "Was it not three men we cast bound into the midst of the fire?" They answered and said to the king, "Certainly, O king." [25] He answered and said, "Look! I see four men loosed *and* walking *about* in the midst of the fire without harm, and the appearance of the fourth is like a son of *the* gods!" [26] Then Nebuchadnezzar came near to the door of the furnace of blazing fire; he responded and said, "Shadrach, Meshach and Abed-nego, come out, you servants of the Most High God, and come here!" Then Shadrach, Meshach and Abed-nego came out of the midst of the fire. [27] And the satraps, the prefects, the governors and the king's high officials gathered around *and* saw in regard to these men that the fire had no effect on the bodies of these men nor was the hair of their head singed, nor were their trousers damaged, nor had the smell of fire *even* come upon them.

[28] Nebuchadnezzar responded and said, "Blessed be the God of Shadrach, Meshach, and Abed-nego, who has sent His angel and delivered His servants who put their trust in Him, violating the king's command, and yielded up their bodies so as not to serve or worship any god except their own God. [29] Therefore, I make a decree that any people, nation or tongue that speaks anything offensive against the God of Shadrach, Meshach and Abed-nego shall be torn limb from limb and their houses reduced to a rubbish heap, inasmuch as there is no other god who is able to deliver in this way." [30] Then the king caused Shadrach, Meshach and Abed-nego to prosper in the province of Babylon.

Introduction

The next four chapters of the book of Daniel are in sharp contrast to the first two. Whereas chapter 2 was distinctly prophetic in character, chapters 3 through 6 appear to be entirely historical in nature. We should bear in mind, however, that even historical passages of the Word of God can have a deeper meaning than meets the eye.

Thus, in Daniel 3-6, although the content of these chapters is historical, their significance is prophetic. In chapter 2 we learned how the great empires of world history would be established; the next question that follows is, how will these empires conduct themselves in their responsibility to the God of heaven? Chapter 2 had shown these empires in their political succession; chapters 3 to 6 will show their moral conduct and character while they rule.

Verse 1: As the chapter begins, we read that Nebuchadnezzar made "an image of gold." In chapter 2, Nebuchadnezzar had worshiped the wisdom of God, as it had been revealed through Daniel. However, he did not profit from the experience as much as he could have, for he failed to repent. Instead, as this chapter opens we find that he has instituted the grossest form of idolatry, and on a grand scale.

The image was doubtless one of Nebuchadnezzar himself. Since Daniel had told the king that, in the vision of the great statue, he was represented by the head of gold, Nebuchadnezzar had his statue made entirely of gold so as to boast of the splendor of his empire. In this way he turned his God-given authority to exalting himself and to insulting the God who made him.

Verse 2: The king decreed that all the nobles of his empire were to gather together for the dedication of his golden image. Nebuchadnezzar recognized, as have many other rulers since his time, that a unifying religion can be a powerful instrument to bind a realm together. Religion, he reasoned, must be made subservient to political aims.

Verse 3: He probably stood before the image to receive their worship and adoration. In situations like this, no crime is greater than nonconformity, yet that is exactly what God asks of us when the things of the world are arrayed against the things of God (Rom. 12:1-2).

Verses 4 and 5: In the clearest possible terms, it is commanded that all shall worship this image. The orchestra is employed to sway everyone's emotions to the same "soulish" mood; as in all idolatrous practices, the senses must be deadened.

It is under these circumstances that idolatry is introduced by the first ruler of the "times of the Gentiles." Rather than recognize his responsibility, Nebuchadnezzar rejects any hint of submission to the God of heaven. Idolatry is spiritual suicide; an idol is nothing in the world, but it is sponsored by demonic activity.

We have said that these historical passages are prophetic as well; this is a case in point. This chapter reveals that just as the "times of the Gentiles" began with idolatry, so they will end. Refer here to Revelation 13:3-8, where the world worships the beast in the last days.

Verse 6: The king's command is to be obeyed; to refuse this idolatry is to burn. Persecution always accompanies the commands of tyrants.

Verse 7: How sad it is that this new, idolatrous worship was so easily instituted and accepted after the events of chapter 2. How easily is man swayed, when far from God!

Verse 8: The Hebrews' refusal to comply could not long escape notice. How easy it would have been to obey! They could have said that they were only complying outwardly while inwardly remaining true to the living God. But no; they would never desert the Lord, even in outward appearance.

The Chaldeans accused the Hebrews, expressed vividly by the original Aramaic, which says "they ate the flesh [or limbs] of the Jews." These accusers were backbiters, a common trait among followers who are spineless themselves. It should also be noticed that Daniel is not included among the accused here, for reasons unknown.

Verses 9 through 12: Notice here that the sore spot for the Chaldeans was the way Nebuchadnezzar had promoted the Hebrews to high office in Babylon. This must have made their refusal all the more galling. The Chaldeans made their accusations broad enough to include the fact that not only did the Hebrews not bow to the image, but they did not worship any of the king's other gods, either.

Verse 13: The king could not allow this defiance to go

unpunished, even though it involved some of the highest officials in his empire. Whenever there is a conflict between politics and religion, there is no accommodation to the rights of conscience before the Lord.

Verse 14: Nebuchadnezzar gave the Hebrews a chance to recant gracefully and escape punishment by obeying his original decree. But spiritual principles are worth all if they are worth anything at all.

Verse 15: The issue was well-defined, and there was no room possible for misunderstanding. Driven by his fury, the king posed a rash question in which he exalted himself—not his gods—above the Lord God. Such challenges are neither unnoticed nor unanswered.

Verse 16: The Hebrews' reply is magnificent beyond expression and has come ringing down through the centuries. They knew that the king was determined in his purpose, and they were steadfast in theirs: there could be no compromise. They had no choice but to obey God rather than men (Acts 5:29).

It was no mean statesman who said that there exists a law higher and greater than the Constitution. Whenever man infringes on the rights and the realm of God, he is stripped of his right to obedience and loyalty.

Verse 17: The Hebrews were not prepared to tell God what their fate should be. If He should grant their deliverance, all was well. If not, God's wisdom was still best (Job 13:15). Their part was to obey God and leave the consequences to Him.

Verse 18: They were respectful to the king, but firm. They had not the slightest idea of obeying his decree. What a testimony these young men were in that day, before all the realm! What a witness has been theirs to all the generations that have followed! This is the purpose for which life is given: to glorify God.

Verse 19: Until now, the king had remained patient. But now that his repeated commands were openly defied, he was beside himself with rage. So great was his anger that his entire appearance was changed. Oh, to be defied this way before all his subjects!

In this senseless rage, Nebuchadnezzar overdid himself. For by heating the furnace seven times hotter than usual, he would actually be decreasing the length of their torment rather than prolonging it.

Verses 20 through 23: There is no question that the heat of the furnace was real, for the men chosen to cast them into it were themselves consumed. As they fell into the furnace, the Hebrew children could well remember the promise of Isaiah 43:2-3:

> When you pass through the waters, I will be with you;
> And through the rivers, they will not overflow you.
> When you walk through the fire, you will not be scorched,
> Nor will the flame burn you.
> For I am the LORD your God,
> The Holy One of Israel, your Savior.

Verse 24: The king was watching from a safe distance, and soon his rage turned to unspeakable astonishment. Before his very eyes he saw those who had been bound, loosed and walking about in the midst of the flame.

Verse 25: In addition to the three Hebrews, Nebuchadnezzar also saw a divine figure in the furnace. Praise God, whenever His children are in the fiery furnace of trials for His name's sake, He is there. Christ never sends forth His sheep unless He goes on before them.

Verse 26: At this, the king called out, "Servants of the Most High God,...come here." Evidently, he acknowledged the supremacy of the God of the Hebrews; but that does not mean he had forsaken his Babylonian gods.

Verse 27: God's protection was complete. Not even a hair was singed on any of the three.

Verse 28: Now that he was in a better frame of mind, Nebuchadnezzar realized that his command was opposed only when he tried to coerce faith. He now respected what the Hebrews' steadfastness of faith had been able to accomplish (Prov. 16:7).

Verse 29: The king then nullified the earlier decree he had issued in his insane pride. The very king who had boasted that no god could deliver from his hand now gave an unsolicited testimony to the power of God.

Verse 30: These young men lost nothing by their faithfulness to God, as their former offices were restored to them.

These men remind us of that faithful remnant in Israel in the coming day of the Tribulation who will defy the insane commands of the beast despite persecution and death (Rev. 12:17). It is blessed indeed to trust our faithful God!

4 The Vision of the Great Tree

Nebuchadnezzar the king to all the peoples, nations, and *men of every* language that live in all the earth: "May your peace abound! ² It has seemed good to me to declare the signs and wonders which the Most High God has done for me.
³ How great are His signs,
And how mighty are His wonders!
His kingdom is an everlasting kingdom,
And His dominion is from generation to generation.
⁴ "I, Nebuchadnezzar, was at ease in my house and flourishing in my palace. ⁵ I saw a dream and it made me fearful; and *these* fantasies *as I lay* on my bed and the visions in my mind kept alarming me. ⁶ So I gave orders to bring into my presence all the wise men of Babylon, that they might make known to me the interpretation of the dream. ⁷ Then the magicians, the conjurers, the Chaldeans, and the diviners came in, and I related the dream to them; but they could not make its interpretation known to me. ⁸ But finally Daniel came in before me, whose name is Belteshazzar according to the name of my god, and in whom is a spirit of the holy gods; and I related the dream to him, *saying*, ⁹ 'O Belteshazzar, chief of the magicians, since I know that a spirit of the holy gods is in you and no mystery baffles you, tell *me* the visions of my dream which I have seen, along with its interpretation. ¹⁰ Now *these were* the visions in my mind *as I lay* on my bed: I was looking, and behold, *there was* a tree in the midst of the earth, and its height *was* great.
¹¹ The tree grew large and became strong,
And its height reached to the sky,
And it *was* visible to the end of the whole earth.
¹² Its foliage *was* beautiful and its fruit abundant,
And in it *was* food for all.

The beasts of the field found shade under it,
And the birds of the sky dwelt in its branches,
And all living creatures fed themselves from it.
[13] "I was looking in the visions in my mind *as I lay* on my bed, and behold, an *angelic* watcher, a holy one, descended from heaven.
[14] He shouted out and spoke as follows:
"Chop down the tree and cut off its branches,
Strip off its foliage and scatter its fruit;
Let the beasts flee from under it,
And the birds from its branches.
[15] Yet leave the stump with its roots in the ground,
But with a band of iron and bronze *around it*
In the new grass of the field;
And let him be drenched with the dew of heaven,
And let him share with the beasts in the grass of the earth.
[16] Let his mind be changed from *that of* a man,
And let a beast's mind be given to him,
And let seven periods of time pass over him.
[17] This sentence is by the decree of the *angelic* watchers,
And the decision is a command of the holy ones,
In order that the living may know
That the Most High is ruler over the realm of mankind,
And bestows it on whom He wishes,
And sets over it the lowliest of men.'"
[18] This is the dream *which* I, King Nebuchadnezzar, have seen. Now you, Belteshazzar, tell *me* its interpretation, inasmuch as none of the wise men of my kingdom is able to make known to me the interpretation; but you are able, for a spirit of the holy gods is in you.'
[19] "Then Daniel, whose name is Belteshazzar, was appalled for a while as his thoughts alarmed him. The king responded and said, 'Belteshazzar, do not let the dream or its interpretation alarm you.' Belteshazzar answered and said, 'My lord, *if only* the dream applied to those who hate you, and its interpretation to your adversaries! [20] The tree that you saw, which became large and grew strong, whose height reached to the sky and was visible to all

the earth, [21] and whose foliage *was* beautiful and its fruit abundant, and in which *was* food for all, under which the beasts of the field dwelt and in whose branches the birds of the sky lodged—[22] it is you, O king; for you have become great and grown strong, and your majesty has become great and reached to the sky and your dominion to the end of the earth. [23] And in that the king saw an *angelic* watcher, a holy one, descending from heaven and saying, "Chop down the tree and destroy it; yet leave the stump with its roots in the ground, but with a band of iron and bronze *around it* in the new grass of the field, and let him be drenched with the dew of heaven, and let him share with the beasts of the field until seven periods of time pass over him"; [24] this is the interpretation, O king, and this is the decree of the Most High, which has come upon my lord the king: [25] that you be driven away from mankind, and your dwelling place be with the beasts of the field, and you be given grass to eat like cattle and be drenched with the dew of heaven; and seven periods of time will pass over you, until you recognize that the Most High is ruler over the realm of mankind, and bestows it on whomever He wishes. [26] And in that it was commanded to leave the stump with the roots of the tree, your kingdom will be assured to you after you recognize that *it is* Heaven *that* rules. [27] Therefore, O king, may my advice be pleasing to you: break away now from your sins by *doing* righteousness, and from your iniquities by showing mercy to *the* poor, in case there may be a prolonging of your prosperity.'

[28] "All *this* happened to Nebuchadnezzar the king. [29] Twelve months later he was walking on the *roof of* the royal palace of Babylon. [30] The king reflected and said, 'Is this not Babylon the great, which I myself have built as a royal residence by the might of my power and for the glory of my majesty?' [31] While the word *was* in the king's mouth, a voice came from heaven, *saying,* 'King Nebuchadnezzar, to you it is declared: sovereignty has been removed from you, [32] and you will be driven away from mankind, and your dwelling place *will be* with the beasts of the field. You will be given grass to eat like cattle, and seven periods of time will pass over you, until you recognize that the Most High is ruler over the realm of mankind and bestows it on whomever He wishes.'

[33] Immediately the word concerning Nebuchadnezzar was fulfilled; and he was driven away from mankind and began eating grass like cattle, and his body was drenched with the dew of heaven, until his hair had grown like eagles' *feathers* and his nails like birds' *claws.*

[34] "But at the end of that period I, Nebuchadnezzar, raised my eyes toward heaven, and my reason returned to me, and I blessed the Most High and praised and honored Him who lives forever;
For His dominion is an everlasting dominion,
And His kingdom *endures* from generation to generation.
[35] And all the inhabitants of the earth are accounted as nothing,
But He does according to His will in the host of heaven
And *among* the inhabitants of earth;
And no one can ward off His hand
Or say to Him, 'What hast Thou done?'
[36] At that time my reason returned to me. And my majesty and splendor were restored to me for the glory of my kingdom, and my counselors and my nobles began seeking me out; so I was reestablished in my sovereignty, and surpassing greatness was added to me. [37] Now I Nebuchadnezzar praise, exalt, and honor the King of heaven, for all His works are true and His ways just, and He is able to humble those who walk in pride."

Introduction

The fourth chapter of the book of Daniel further describes the way in which emperors rule during the "times of the Gentiles." In particular, it demonstrates how God punished King Nebuchadnezzar for his pride by afflicting him with insanity. The king is reduced to the level of the beasts of the field, thus illustrating the truth of Psalm 49:6, 10-12.

Evidently, the vision of the great image (chap. 2) was not enough to put Nebuchadnezzar into right relationship with the Lord, for the Lord then sent another dream to the king in an effort to turn him from his godless ways. Job 33:14-18 describes how God uses dreams to speak to men who have no other source of divine revelation. In this case, God used the vision of the great tree to speak to the king's heart.

We should remember that this chapter of Scripture was written by King Nebuchadnezzar himself and was preserved by Daniel under the direction of the Holy Spirit. According to the pagan historian Abydenus (c. 268 B.C.), the events of this chapter occurred after Nebuchadnezzar's campaign victories and after he had built his new palace in only fifteen days.

This is the account of the way God brought this proud king to humble himself before Him, the story of his conversion. It shows how real was the movement of the Spirit of God in this heathen's soul. It represents the way in which world rulers can be alienated from God; how they become degraded and beastly in character; and how they shall all be brought into submission to God at the end of time, when Christ returns in His glory.

Verse 1: This account is especially moving, for it is the personal testimony of a man who was the greatest monarch of his day, sovereign of all the peoples of the earth. His salutation was the usual one in the ancient Near East, where peace was so highly prized that it found its way into every greeting.

Verse 2: Having received the instruction of God, the king was not slow to tell others of the marvelous workings of His grace. Testimony like this always brings praise to God and strength to those who hear it (cf. Psalm 107:1-3).

Verse 3: He had hoped that his own kingdom might be eternal, but now Nebuchadnezzar realized that only the Kingdom of God can last forever. Eternity is never within man's limited grasp; it can only be attained by God.

Verse 4: The king described his condition before the Lord began to deal with him. It was a condition characteristic of so many of the unsaved, a false sense of security. Do not rely on such a feeling yourself. If the king is ever to know life and blessing, the Lord must first rouse him from his complacency.

Verse 5: As had happened earlier (2:1), the king saw a dream that greatly troubled and frightened him. That was its purpose.

Verse 6: Since he had wise men to meet this kind of need, Nebuchadnezzar immediately turned to them for help. Their first failure to interpret his dreams evidently had not impressed him. It is always natural for one to seek help on his own level rather than turn to God; but these wise men were helpless to explain this dream, as well.

Notice, too, that this case was different from the one in chapter 2, when the king had forgotten his dream. He remembered this one, but its meaning was still beyond the comprehension of the Chaldeans. God alone is able to reveal the truth of his warnings to the king.

Verses 7 and 8: As in thousands of other instances, man's extremity is God's opportunity. When all others failed, the king finally turned to Daniel. Calling on Daniel as a last resort surely served to impress the king's heart with the helplessness of man—and the ability of the man to whom God revealed truth.

Verse 9: Nebuchadnezzar referred here to Daniel as "chief of the magicians," one who could explain the mysteries that baffled everyone else. To him, the living God of Daniel was just another god in his realm. Notice that he said, "A spirit of the holy *gods* is in you" (emphasis added). The king continued to think and speak like a heathen.

Verse 10: The figures employed by the Holy Spirit are always significant. This time it was neither the figure of a man nor that of a beast—as in chapter 7—but the figure of a flourishing tree. From such passages as Ezekiel 31:3 and Matthew 13:31-32, we learn that a tree symbolizes earthly greatness, grandeur, and power.

The tree in the king's vision was in a most conspicuous place, the very middle of the earth, and its height was impressive. This symbolized King Nebuchadnezzar, whose lines of power went out to all the known inhabited earth.

Verse 11: As it grew, this tree came to cast its shadow over all the earth.

Verse 12: This verse intimates why God establishes earthly kings and rulers. It is for the protection and refuge of all creatures, man, beast, and bird alike.

Verse 13: The holy angels are entrusted with the task of watching over earthly kingdoms and carrying out God's commands with respect to them (cf. chap. 10).

Verses 14 and 15: The awe-inspiring sentence is pronounced here, yet provision is made for the continuation of his rule: the tree stump is left rooted to the earth.

Verse 16: Here we are definitely told that the figure of the tree has represented a man all along. This was the most severe part of Nebuchadnezzar's sentence: the source of his pride, his reason, would be unseated. He was to become like the beasts of the field, smitten with what is known as lycanthropy.

What depths are reached when man refuses to recognize his proper place before God! This passage clearly teaches that when men abdicate their responsibility before God, they become deranged. This condition that had been predicted for the king would last for "seven times," or, as it is generally understood, seven years.

Verse 17: God does nothing capriciously, and His purpose in humbling the king was now revealed. Mankind must know that rule and power are not native to man but are delegated by God, who is the ultimate ruler of all. This is political science of the highest order.

Verse 18: Although all the king's other wise men had failed him, he still showed great confidence in Daniel's ability.

Verse 19: This verse reveals the heart of Daniel as well as

any in the entire book of Daniel. He knew the meaning of
this dream and how well Nebuchadnezzar deserved what
was to come upon him. Nevertheless, Daniel's heart was
concerned for the king and grieved over what he had to tell
him. This was the distinctive feature of the true prophets of
God: though they often had to predict judgments, they were
nevertheless grieved when any of God's creatures were
chastised.

In this verse, Daniel said he wished that this dream and its
interpretation applied to the king's enemies and not to the
king, so dreadful was its meaning. By saying this, Daniel
offered an expression of his personal loyalty to the king and
of his concern for the king's continued well-being.

Verses 20 through 22: Daniel now turned to the interpretation of the king's dream. The tree, said Daniel, represented the king himself in all his greatness. Nebuchadnezzar
had reached the peak of his political power. He possessed
Armenia in the north, as well as a large portion of Asia
Minor. In the west, he ruled Syria and, at one time, Egypt as
well. Toward the south, his power reached the Persian Gulf.
In the east, the Medes and Elamites were under his rule.

Verses 23 and 24: In verse 17, Nebuchadnezzar's fate had
been referred to as "the decree of the angelic watchers."
Here Daniel called it the decree of the Most High. It is God
who commands; angels are but His ministers (Heb. 1:13-14).

Verse 25: When the tree was cut down, it meant that the
king was to be humbled and driven from human society as if
he were an animal. He was to live among the beasts of the
field, eating their food and exhibiting their behavior. This
contrast between the life of beasts and the life of men is an
important one, for it provides the key to interpreting the
symbolism found in chapter 7.

The king's condition was to continue until he realized the
mighty hand of God in his rule and acknowledged that God
freely chooses to give rule to whomever He pleases.

Verse 26: The stump of the tree was allowed to remain, and this signifies that Nebuchadnezzar was not to lose his kingdom forever. God would restore rule to the Babylonian monarch in His good time.

Verse 27: Before Daniel concluded, he faithfully counseled the king for his own welfare. He entreated Nebuchadnezzar to forsake his sins for righteousness, his iniquity for mercy.

This is not counsel to earn salvation by works. Rather, Daniel appealed to the king to turn to God's righteousness and manifest this change in his lifestyle. If he were to do so, it was possible that God's judgment could be averted and the king's well-being prolonged.

Verse 28: Daniel's timely warning went unheeded, and all that he had predicted was fulfilled in the life of King Nebuchadnezzar.

Verses 29 and 30: Why had all this come upon Nebuchadnezzar? Of what did his sin consist? He prided himself on the accomplishments of his realm and utterly ignored the claims of God on his life. He refused to recognize his debt to God for all that he had. The study of ancient history confirms that he had indeed beautified and adorned the old city of Babylon with high walls and a magnificent palace.

Verse 31: Because in God's sight Nebuchadnezzar seemed to be more than a mere man, his punishment was to become less than fully human. All connection with God was lost; he now had no more concept of God than a beast of the field.

Verse 32: The king became a miserable spectacle, not even fit to live among his own subjects. In the Oriental countries of those days, the insane were thought to be afflicted by God Himself and were allowed to wander wherever they wished.

What a picture this is of world powers going their own proud way and then enduring the judgment of beastly dictators. It is madness of the worst sort to spurn the clear word of God and to refuse God the honor rightfully due Him;

sadly, such has been the course of nations during the "times of the Gentiles." What happened to Nebuchadnezzar was not confined to him alone; it has been repeated many times over the centuries.

Verse 33: It is generally agreed that this disorder was a mania known as lycanthropy. The Babylonian historian Berosus confirms that Nebuchadnezzar suffered from an illness at this time, and inscriptions indicate that this was a period during which the king carried out no great public works.

Verse 34: The first symptom of Nebuchadnezzar's recovery was that he raised his eyes toward heaven, the opposite of the habit of beasts. He had been allowed to suffer the full time of his sentence; his training period was now over. His eyes, which for seven long years had seen only the earth before them, now turned to recognize the God they had defied so long ago.

The ability to recognize God is the fundamental difference between beasts and men. In any age, the glory of man is to recognize God and to take his place relative to the Sovereign of the universe.

The king returned to Him who smote him. His words were now words of praise and adoration of the God who corrects and chastens even the mightiest on earth. The God whom he had not honored before, he now honored. He was now quite prepared to acknowledge the temporary nature of man's dominion, which serves to highlight the eternal dominion of God.

Verse 35: Compared to the power of God, the nations of the world are as nothing. As Isaiah 40:15 and 17 describe, the Lord overrules in every realm—in heaven, on earth, and under the earth—in order to bring to pass His holy will:

> Behold, the nations are like a drop from a bucket,
> And are regarded as a speck of dust on the scales;
> Behold, He lifts up the islands like fine dust....

All the nations are as nothing before Him,
They are regarded by Him as less than nothing
and meaningless.

Verse 36: According to one inscription, Nebuchadnezzar ceased for a time to build or to maintain his kingdom. There is no other instance in ancient Near Eastern history of a king recording his own inactivity.

As soon as the king's eyes were turned to God and he praised the Lord, his counselors sought him out and restored him to the throne. On previous occasions, Nebuchadnezzar had bowed down before Daniel and had sweet fragrances offered to him. He had also decreed that the God of the Jews was to be worshiped by all his subjects, as though to add yet another god to the many gods of the Babylonians.

Now, however, he behaved differently. The king turned aside from all other gods and bowed down before the Lord alone. Significantly, Nebuchadnezzar was now more interested in his own relationship to the Lord than in commanding the religious beliefs of others.

Verse 37: The king of Babylon was unceasing in his praise of the King of heaven. He showed by this testimony that he recognized his true position in relation to the Ruler of the universe.

Notice that Nebuchadnezzar admitted that all God's ways are just. Whatever he was called upon to endure, he deserved all of it. He was prepared to condemn himself so that God would be justified (cf. Job 40:8). He now knew the devastating price of pride.

This king is an outstanding example for all the world to see. He had surely been brought to a blessed state, but at what a price!

5 The Handwriting on the Wall

Belshazzar the king held a great feast for a thousand of his nobles, and he was drinking wine in the presence of the thousand. ² When Belshazzar tasted the wine, he gave orders to bring the gold and silver vessels which Nebuchadnezzar his father had taken out of the temple which *was* in Jerusalem, in order that the king and his nobles, his wives, and his concubines might drink from them. ³ Then they brought the gold vessels that had been taken out of the temple, the house of God which *was* in Jerusalem; and the king and his nobles, his wives, and his concubines drank from them. ⁴ They drank the wine and praised the gods of gold and silver, of bronze, iron, wood, and stone.

⁵ Suddenly the fingers of a man's hand emerged and began writing opposite the lampstand on the plaster of the wall of the king's palace, and the king saw the back of the hand that did the writing. ⁶ Then the king's face grew pale, and his thoughts alarmed him; and his hip joints went slack, and his knees began knocking together. ⁷ The king called aloud to bring in the conjurers, the Chaldeans and the diviners. The king spoke and said to the wise men of Babylon, "Any man who can read this inscription and explain its interpretation to me will be clothed with purple, and *have* a necklace of gold around his neck, and have authority as third *ruler* in the kingdom." ⁸ Then all the king's wise men came in, but they could not read the inscription or make known its interpretation to the king. ⁹ Then King Belshazzar was greatly alarmed, his face grew *even* paler, and his nobles were perplexed.

¹⁰ The queen entered the banquet hall because of the words of the king and his nobles; the queen spoke and said, "O king, live forever! Do not let your thoughts alarm you or your face be pale. ¹¹ There is a man in your kingdom in whom is a spirit of the holy

gods; and in the days of your father, illumination, insight, and wisdom like the wisdom of the gods were found in him. And King Nebuchadnezzar, your father, your father the king, appointed him chief of the magicians, conjurers, Chaldeans, *and* diviners. ¹² *This was* because an extraordinary spirit, knowledge and insight, interpretation of dreams, explanation of enigmas, and solving of difficult problems were found in this Daniel, whom the king named Belteshazzar. Let Daniel now be summoned, and he will declare the interpretation."

¹³ Then Daniel was brought in before the king. The king spoke and said to Daniel, "Are you that Daniel who is one of the exiles from Judah, whom my father the king brought from Judah? ¹⁴ Now I have heard about you that a spirit of the gods is in you, and that illumination, insight, and extraordinary wisdom have been found in you. ¹⁵ Just now the wise men *and* the conjurers were brought in before me that they might read this inscription and make its interpretation known to me, but they could not declare the interpretation of the message. ¹⁶ But I personally have heard about you, that you are able to give interpretations and solve difficult problems. Now if you are able to read the inscription and make its interpretation known to me, you will be clothed with purple and *wear* a necklace of gold around your neck, and you will have authority as the third *ruler* in the kingdom."

¹⁷ Then Daniel answered and said before the king, "Keep your gifts for yourself, or give your rewards to someone else; however, I will read the inscription to the king and make the interpretation known to him. ¹⁸ O king, the Most High God granted sovereignty, grandeur, glory, and majesty to Nebuchadnezzar your father. ¹⁹ And because of the grandeur which He bestowed on him, all the peoples, nations, and *men of every* language feared and trembled before him; whomever he wished he killed, and whomever he wished he spared alive; and whomever he wished he elevated, and whomever he wished he humbled. ²⁰ But when his heart was lifted up and his spirit became so proud that he behaved arrogantly, he was deposed from his royal throne, and *his* glory was taken away from him. ²¹ He was also driven away from mankind, and his heart was made like *that of* beasts, and his dwelling place *was* with the wild donkeys. He was given grass to eat like cattle, and his body

was drenched with the dew of heaven, until he recognized that the Most High God is ruler over the realm of mankind, and *that* He sets over it whomever He wishes. [22] Yet you, his son, Belshazzar, have not humbled your heart, even though you knew all this, [23] but you have exalted yourself against the Lord of heaven; and they have brought the vessels of His house before you, and you and your nobles, your wives and your concubines have been drinking wine from them; and you have praised the gods of silver and gold, of bronze, iron, wood and stone, which do not see, hear or understand. But the God in whose hand are your life-breath and your ways, you have not glorified. [24] Then the hand was sent from Him, and this inscription was written out.

[25] "Now this is the inscription that was written out: 'MENĒ, MENĒ, TEKĒL, UPHARSIN.' [26] This is the interpretation of the message: "MENĒ'—God has numbered your kingdom and put an end to it. [27] "TEKĒL—you have been weighed on the scales and found deficient. [28] "PERĒS'—your kingdom has been divided and given over to the Medes and Persians."

[29] Then Belshazzar gave orders, and they clothed Daniel with purple and *put* a necklace of gold around his neck, and issued a proclamation concerning him that he *now* had authority as the third *ruler* in the kingdom.

[30] That same night Belshazzar the Chaldean king was slain. [31] So Darius the Mede received the kingdom at about the age of sixty-two.

Introduction

If the student of the Word of God has been disappointed in the conduct of world monarchs during the "times of the Gentiles," he has not yet reached the end of this sad tale. Their usual pattern is to first commit idolatry and defy His claims on their individual consciences. Next, they usually become deranged in their pride, and they fail to recognize the authority of God in worldly affairs.

Now, in chapter 5, we see yet another phase of the

conduct of world powers during the "times of the Gentiles." More than a quarter of a century has elapsed between the events described in chapters 4 and 5. Nebuchadnezzar died after a reign of forty-four years, in 561 B.C.

His son, Evil-merodach, succeeded to the throne of the Babylonian Empire. The Bible refers to Evil-merodach in 2 Kings 25:27-30. In examining this passage, it has been assumed that Evil-merodach's actions are to be understood as acts of kindness toward the Jews, which he performed out of regard for his father—and because of the wonderful way the God of Israel had dealt with Israel. Evil-merodach reigned only two years, for he was assassinated in a revolt led by his brother-in-law, Neriglissar (559 B.C.). Neriglissar's rule was equally brief, and his son, Labashi Marduk, reigned for less than a year.

In 555 B.C., Nabonidus usurped the throne. He was the father of Belshazzar and was ruler of Babylon in 538 B.C., when it fell to the Medes and Persians under Cyrus. Because of his frequent military campaigns in the west, Nabonidus left the rule of his empire in the hands of his son, Belshazzar. It seems most likely that Belshazzar was related to Nebuchadnezzar through his mother. Thus, in this chapter, we near the end of the empire represented by the head of gold in the great statue described in chapter 2.

Verse 1: At the very hour Belshazzar held his feast, his capital of Babylon was under siege by Cyrus the Persian. Since he had abundant food and provisions in the city, Belshazzar seems to have cared little for the besiegers. This was probably an annual feast day held in honor of some of the Babylonian deities.

This verse refers to the feast's being attended by "a thousand of his nobles." Although this was long thought to be an exaggeration, excavations in Babylon have established that such a number may indeed be reasonable. One historian estimates that one Persian king furnished daily provisions for 15,000 men, and another reports that Alexander the Great hosted 10,000 men at one of his festivals.

As Belshazzar's guests were feasting, they drank as well. The king himself ate and drank in the presence of his nobles, which was unusual; the custom was for the king to eat and drink separately (cf. Esther 1:3; Jeremiah 52:33). Here, however, the king drank wine in public, and, from all appearances, he drank it to great excess.

Verse 2: While under the wine's influence, Belshazzar did something he probably would not have done in more sober moments: "He gave orders to bring the gold and silver vessels which Nebuchadnezzar his father had taken out of the temple which was in Jerusalem." These had evidently been stored in the palace as cherished trophies of conquest, and now the king wanted to display them and have his guests drink from them.

What made Belshazzar think of the Lord in the midst of this revelry? It could have been a drunken fancy; it could be that he had been warned of the prophecies of Babylon's doom. Whatever the cause, there is no doubt that Belshazzar's act was one of open defiance of God. That such holy vessels, dedicated to the worship and service of the true God, should be so openly desecrated strikes the reverent reader of Scripture with astonishment. When men are beside themselves, nothing is too sacred to be profaned.

Verse 3: They did drink from the sacred vessels. This was an impudence of vast proportions and was more than enough to call down the judgment of Almighty God.

Verse 4: The fact that they drank from these vessels is repeated to emphasize the heinousness of the deed. What was worse, in their drunken revelry they heaped praise upon their man-made, worthless gods. This was adding insult to injury! How low can man stoop, how ripe for judgment can the human heart become?

Have you noticed how in recent years the world has

stepped into the "sanctuary" of faith and laid its ruthless hands on some of the things we hold most sacred? Our day has seen this impious sacrilege carried into many other realms, as well. Is God unmindful of this? Will He not visit for such defiance?

Verse 5: In that very hour, the visitation of God's judgment was made manifest, as there suddenly appeared the fingers of a man's hand, writing on the wall.

The sight was alarming, for no human being could claim to have done this. The hand appeared opposite the lamp-stand making it all the more clearly visible. And on the wall where the king would ordinarily read inscriptions describing his greatness, he now would read an inscription describing his doom.

Verse 6: The king's expression, which had reflected nothing but hilarity a moment before, was suddenly drained to a deathly pallor. Even before he knew the full import of this new message, his thoughts alarmed him and he was filled with fear.

Belshazzar's terror was described as vividly as Daniel could relate it. "His hip joints went slack, and his knees began knocking together." A moment before, the drunken king had felt brave enough to hurl insults into the face of the living God; but with the flick of a hand, the Lord had reduced him to a quivering mass of terror.

Verse 7: Belshazzar was so fear-stricken that he cried out with all his might for his astrologers. Again, he sought out men as his first resort, and God was left out of the picture; how the world loves to be deceived! It repeatedly closes its eyes to the clear sunlight of God's truth.

To hasten the interpretation of the handwriting on the wall, the king offered the third place in the kingdom to whoever could explain it. One can appreciate how much importance he attached to this sign by realizing that Belshazzar and his father held the first two places in the kingdom; the third place was thus the highest position attainable for any other man.

Verse 8: It has been said that the handwriting on the wall was written in some strange or supernatural script, so that the otherwise literate wise men could not decipher it. We understand the case to be otherwise.

It would appear that they could read the actual message: "MENĒ, MENĒ, TEKĒL, UPHARSHIN." That is clear enough Aramaic, but they could not understand the meaning or significance of the words. For example, a small child could read "H₂O" with no trouble, but he probably could not understand that it signifies water. So it was with these wise men; they could read what the words said, but they could not explain what they meant.

Verse 9: Now the king was more troubled than ever. What could be the meaning of this strange message? His heart warned him that it promised him no good. Belshazzar's appearance grew worse: this was maddening! Even his nobles stood in amazement. They were soon to learn that they, too, were approaching their destruction.

Verse 10: At this tense juncture, the Queen Mother stepped in. She was doubtless the widow of Nebuchadnezzar.

Verse 11: She counseled the king not to be alarmed, for the man was at hand to solve the mystery. She not only remembered Daniel, but she also remembered all his dealings with her deceased husband, Nebuchadnezzar. She praised his wisdom, which was indirect praise of the revelation of God, and so set forth his qualifications that the king could now consult him with confidence.

Verse 12: Inasmuch as Daniel was distinguished by his excellent mind, his ability to interpret dreams, and his understanding of enigmas, the king did not need to hesitate in calling him and laying before him the problem at hand. It would seem, from all appearances, that Daniel was no longer employed at court. It was only the Queen Mother who knew of him and how he could be reached.

Verse 13: When Daniel was brought before the king, probably from somewhere in the city of Babylon, Belshazzar knew very little about him and had to inquire whether Daniel was one of the captives from Judah.

Verse 14: The king now repeated the Queen Mother's recommendation of Daniel.

Verse 15: The king was hampered by the helplessness of his counselors. Just as the race is not always to the swift, so the solution of problems is not always to the worldly wise.

Verse 16: Belshazzar now offered Daniel the reward he had originally promised to whoever could interpret the handwriting.

Verse 17: Daniel's answer was not intended as a rebuff or as an insult to the king. Rather, he was merely stating that he sought no reward. Daniel was not moved by personal desires in this matter, for he had not presented himself: the king had summoned him.

Verse 18: Daniel's reference to Nebuchadnezzar was probably meant to show the king the difference between his famous grandfather and himself. He should have learned how God would deal with him from the clear way He had dealt with Nebuchadnezzar before him.

It appears Belshazzar had learned little from history. It pays to learn well the lessons God has written so clearly in His providential dealings with mankind. In this case, God was the sole source of Nebuchadnezzar's honor and glory.

Verse 19: Daniel next described how comprehensive was Nebuchadnezzar's power; he had been an absolute monarch, with all nations under his command. He had the power of life and death over his subjects, and it was his prerogative to elevate to high office or to remove.

Verses 20 and 21: For all his power, however, even Nebuchadnezzar could not escape the consequences of the sin of pride. This refers to the events described in chapter 4.

Verse 22: Knowing his family history, Belshazzar should have walked in humility before the Lord. One of the most amazing spectacles in this world is how little men really profit from the judgments of God.

Verse 23: Belshazzar had defied the very Lord of heaven, who had rebuked and humbled Nebuchadnezzar. An arrogant spirit of defiance had characterized Belshazzar throughout his reign, but this was its blasphemous climax. The king seems not to have realized that he depended on God to give him the very breath with which he blasphemed.

Verses 24 and 25: The handwriting on the wall was actually three words, with the first repeated: "MENE, MENE, TEKEL, UPHARSIN."

Verse 26: In the next three verses, Daniel interpreted the handwriting on the wall. "MENE" means "numbering"; "TEKEL" means "to weigh"; "UPHARSIN" means "to divide." If that is the meaning of these three words, what message were they intended to convey?

Their interpretation required divine disclosure and revelation. The first portion of the message, "MENE, MENE," meant that the days of the Babylonian Empire were numbered. It is interesting that Daniel did not say that the days of the *king* were numbered (although they were), only that the days of the *kingdom* were. This empire's doom had been pronounced; it soon would fall.

Verse 27: The second portion of the message, "TEKEL," meant that the kingdom itself had been placed in the divine balances—as if to determine its worth—and had been found deficient. The ancient Egyptians believed that the god Osiris weighed the deeds of the dead in a literal balance; perhaps the Babylonians believed in the same idea. If they did, this judgment would be especially pointed.

In 1 Samuel 2:3 it is written, "The LORD is a God of

knowledge, and with Him actions are weighed." God had weighed Belshazzar in the scale of moral value to find his real worth and had found him too light: there was no true value there.

Verse 28: Lastly, the third portion of the divine message, "UPHARSIN," meant that Belshazzar's Babylonian Empire was to be divided among the Medes and the Persians. It is interesting that the words for "divide" and "Persians" are very similar. This prophecy was literally fulfilled when Cyrus conquered the great Babylonian Empire and established the Medo-Persian Empire in its place.

Verse 29: The king rewarded Daniel exactly as he promised he would, despite the ominous message he brought—and despite the fact that at this late hour, honors conferred by this king would not be worth much. This is a remarkable example of the result of faithfulness: Daniel did his duty, and God saw that he was rewarded for it.

Verse 30: That same night, so soon after the judgment was pronounced, its provisions were fulfilled. Belshazzar was slain, and the connection between his sin and his fall was inescapable.

Cyrus the Persian showed great military prowess. He diverted the Euphrates River into a new channel and marched his army into Babylon through the dry riverbed while the Babylonians were still carousing.

Verse 31: Although the city was actually taken by Cyrus, it was done in the name of Cyrus's uncle, Darius the Mede. Thus Babylon came to a disgraceful end when it impiously laid its hands on the sacred vessels of God. Remember, God has means of bringing the proudest down to destruction.

6 Daniel in the Lions' Den

It seemed good to Darius to appoint 120 satraps over the kingdom, that they should be in charge of the whole kingdom, ² and over them three commissioners (of whom Daniel was one), that these satraps might be accountable to them, and that the king might not suffer loss. ³ Then this Daniel began distinguishing himself among the commissioners and satraps because he possessed an extraordinary spirit, and the king planned to appoint him over the entire kingdom. ⁴ Then the commissioners and satraps began trying to find a ground of accusation against Daniel in regard to government affairs; but they could find no ground of accusation or *evidence of* corruption, inasmuch as he was faithful, and no negligence or corruption was *to be* found in him. ⁵ Then these men said, "We shall not find any ground of accusation against this Daniel unless we find *it* against him with regard to the law of his God." ⁶ Then these commissioners and satraps came by agreement to the king and spoke to him as follows: "King Darius, live forever! ⁷ All the commissioners of the kingdom, the prefects and the satraps, the high officials and the governors have consulted together that the king should establish a statute and enforce an injunction that anyone who makes a petition to any god or man besides you, O king, for thirty days, shall be cast into the lions' den. ⁸ Now, O king, establish the injunction and sign the document so that it may not be changed, according to the law of the Medes and Persians, which may not be revoked." ⁹ Therefore King Darius signed the document, that is, the injunction.

¹⁰ Now when Daniel knew that the document was signed, he entered his house (now in his roof chamber he had windows open toward Jerusalem); and he continued kneeling on his knees three times a day, praying and giving thanks before his God, as he had

71

been doing previously. ¹¹ Then these men came by agreement and found Daniel making petition and supplication before his God. ¹² Then they approached and spoke before the king about the king's injunction, "Did you not sign an injunction that any man who makes a petition to any god or man besides you, O king, for thirty days, is to be cast into the lions' den?" The king answered and said, "The statement is true, according to the law of the Medes and Persians, which may not be revoked." ¹³ Then they answered and spoke before the king, "Daniel, who is one of the exiles from Judah, pays no attention to you, O king, or to the injunction which you signed, but keeps making his petition three times a day." ¹⁴ Then, as soon as the king heard this statement, he was deeply distressed and set *his* mind on delivering Daniel; and even until sunset he kept exerting himself to rescue him. ¹⁵ Then these men came by agreement to the king and said to the king, "Recognize, O king, that it is a law of the Medes and Persians that no injunction or statute which the king establishes may be changed."

¹⁶ Then the king gave orders, and Daniel was brought in and cast into the lions' den. The king spoke and said to Daniel, "Your God whom you constantly serve will Himself deliver you." ¹⁷ And a stone was brought and laid over the mouth of the den; and the king sealed it with his own signet ring and with the signet rings of his nobles, so that nothing might be changed in regard to Daniel. ¹⁸ Then the king went off to his palace and spent the night fasting, and no entertainment was brought before him; and his sleep fled from him.

¹⁹ Then the king arose with the dawn, at the break of day, and went in haste to the lions' den. ²⁰ And when he had come near the den to Daniel, he cried out with a troubled voice. The king spoke and said to Daniel, "Daniel, servant of the living God, has your God, whom you constantly serve, been able to deliver you from the lions?" ²¹ Then Daniel spoke to the king, "O king, live forever! ²² My God sent His angel and shut the lions' mouths, and they have not harmed me, inasmuch as I was found innocent before Him; and also toward you, O king, I have committed no crime." ²³ Then the king was very pleased and gave orders for Daniel to be taken up out of the den. So Daniel was taken up out of the den, and no injury whatever was found on him, because he had trusted in his

God. [24] The king then gave orders, and they brought those men who had maliciously accused Daniel, and they cast them, their children, and their wives into the lions' den; and they had not reached the bottom of the den before the lions overpowered them and crushed all their bones.

[25] Then Darius the king wrote to all the peoples, nations, and *men of every* language who were living in all the land: "May your peace abound! [26] I make a decree that in all the dominion of my kingdom men are to fear and tremble before the God of Daniel;
For He is the living God and enduring forever,
And His kingdom is one which will not be destroyed,
And His dominion *will be* forever.
[27] He delivers and rescues and performs signs and wonders
In heaven and on earth,
Who has *also* delivered Daniel from the power of the lions."
[28] So this Daniel enjoyed success in the reign of Darius and in the reign of Cyrus the Persian.

Introduction

The iniquity of world rulers during the "times of the Gentiles" has not yet been examined to the last detail. These monarchs have sponsored idolatry in the past, and they will again in the prophetic future. They became deranged by their senseless, overbearing pride in the past, and they will again in the predicted future. They were blatantly impious in their desecration of holy things in the past, and they will be again in the foretold future.

The Antichrist will so profane the sanctuary of God that it will be in that very place that he will sit and claim divine honors (2 Thess. 2:3-12). But that is not all; there is yet a final touch. Man will finally seek to displace God altogether.

When Nebuchadnezzar commanded his subjects to worship his image, he did not forbid them to worship any other gods; he himself worshiped many gods. But Darius the Mede went far beyond that. He forbade on pain of death any petition to the living God: all prayer was to be directed to him! This demanded that the inalienable and inviolable rights of God be given to a lowly man.

Verse 1: Since the Babylonian Empire had now been annexed to the Medo-Persian Empire as a subject kingdom, the Persians needed to establish rulers over the conquered territories. These would need to be men of great reliability and integrity.

Verse 2: Different ranks of officers were to be appointed, with Daniel the highest of all. His position in the former kingdom had established his reputation, and now he was charged with the oversight of the empire to assure that the king would suffer no losses of any kind.

Verse 3: King Darius recognized Daniel's ability and so decided to promote him to oversee the entire empire. As soon as this became known to the other high officials, they determined to ruin him.

Verse 4: Daniel's enemies thus sought some pretext whereby he could be discredited. Such court intrigue has been known in every kingdom and every age, and Daniel must have been well aware of it. For their part, Daniel's enemies were well aware that he was a foreigner and of a captive people.

They sought some fault in him, which they could then frame as neglect of duty, abuse of power, or maladministration. It is a splendid testimony to Daniel that they could find no grounds on which to accuse him. His life had been exemplary.

Verse 5: These jealous plotters concluded that the only way they could accuse Daniel would be on religious grounds. Their purpose would be achieved if they could only make his religious beliefs appear to be in conflict with loyalty to the king. They planned their trap meticulously and counted on Daniel to remain true to his God at any cost.

The Jews' religion had never been declared illegal; and to

have asked King Darius to declare it so would have exposed their design. So, they finally settled on a plan that would be most likely to succeed, based as it was on the king's vanity, and that would outwardly appear to be no more than a simple test of loyalty for all his subjects.

The king fell into their trap and signed the decree. He should have asked himself, "Why all this sudden show of loyalty to me? Why isn't Daniel among those who propose this law? What would the long-term results of this be? Do the officers who propose it have any ulterior motives?" But flattery was stronger than reflection in this case, and the outrage was committed.

Verses 6 and 7: The decree itself would have to be made by the king, but it was evidently the custom for high government officials to initiate and recommend legislation. In this case, they couched the terms of the decree in the broadest language possible. The decree was that "anyone who makes a petition to any god or man besides you, O king, for thirty days, shall be cast into the lion's den."

The thirty-day time limit would be sufficient for their purposes; in that time, they should be able to collect evidence against Daniel. To have made the decree apply for any longer than thirty days might have aroused the opposition of the people at large, and enforcement would have become impossible.

It should be noted that the mention of lions here provides incidental evidence of the genuineness of the book of Daniel. The Persians would never execute people by fire, as Nebuchadnezzar the Babylonian had in chapter 3, for they were fire-worshipers. They thus had to resort to other means of execution, as is confirmed by this passage.

Verses 8 and 9: When the king signed the decree, it became the irrevocable law of the realm. The fact that it was irrevocable is peculiar to Medo-Persian culture and stems from the fact that the monarch was considered infallible. Therefore, because he never made mistakes, there was never need to change any decree he issued. The king himself could not change one of his own edicts (cf. Esther 1:19).

The fact that the Medes are named before the Persians in this account is yet another indication of the historical accuracy of this book, for although Cyrus the Persian exercised more control over the daily affairs of government, he reigned subordinate to Darius the Mede. After Darius's death, their order of precedence was reversed.

Verse 10: When Daniel found out about the new decree, he went home to pray in his accustomed manner. His open window was not intended as a defiant display but was intended to direct his attention to the holy city, Jerusalem. All Jews in exile—even today—face toward Jerusalem in prayer. This is in keeping with the prayer of King Solomon at the dedication of the temple (1 Kings 8:44-49); and the upper room was the customary prayer chamber for the Jews (cf. Mark 14:12-16; Acts 1:13).

Daniel took the supplicant's normal position on his knees and observed his fixed habit of praying three times each day. This was not done out of contempt or disloyalty to the king; Daniel simply believed that no earthly ruler dared to intervene in the relationship between a man and his God. Thus, the king's edict had no effect on Daniel's spiritual life: he continued just as he always had.

Verse 11: Daniel's enemies broke in upon him, hastily violating the privacy of his devotions. In this way they sought to catch him in the very act of prayer to God—and defiance of the king.

Verse 12: They lost no time in bringing their accusation before the king. First, they were careful to remind the king of the decree he had issued. Darius reaffirmed the edict, never dreaming that the third man in all the kingdom was about to be condemned by it. Daniel's enemies thus sprang the trap they had so carefully prepared.

Verse 13: Daniel's accusers referred to him contemptuously, in a manner calculated to emphasize his foreign origin. A foreigner elevated to such a high post in the kingdom should be among the most loyal to the king, they said, but Daniel disregarded the king's will by his disobedience. We would say that he did not regard Darius, because he did regard the living God.

Verse 14: Darius was very unhappy with himself for having issued the decree so hastily. At this point, he may not have known that the law was originally aimed at Daniel. In any event, he was caught in a dilemma: he esteemed Daniel highly, yet the decree was irrevocable. The king sought any loophole whereby Daniel could be saved, but he was trapped by his own decree.

Verse 15: Daniel's enemies were taking no chances: they could not allow the king to change his mind or reduce Daniel's punishment. Daniel had to be done away with as soon as possible, and the best way to accomplish that was to stress the irrevocability of the law.

Verse 16: It was their custom to execute sentence upon a criminal on the same day it was pronounced. This explains why the king so earnestly sought to escape the terms of his own decree. Since the heathen commonly believed that the gods intervened on the behalf of the righteous, Darius expressed the hope that Daniel's God, whom he regarded as *a god*, but not as *the God,* might deliver him. If any god would intervene for a worthy man, he would for Daniel.

Verse 17: Apparently, the power of the king was not what it had been in the days of Nebuchadnezzar, for Darius's power was definitely limited by the nobility. The seals of the nobles guaranteed that the king had fulfilled the provisions of the law, whereas Darius's seal guaranteed that if Daniel were somehow to survive the lions, he would not be put to death some other way.

Verse 18: The king knew that he had been party to a serious injustice, and it lay heavily on his conscience. He neither ate nor drank nor slept that night.

Verse 19: Having spent such a long night fasting and burdened with remorse, the king could contain his sense of suspense no longer; he must know whether Daniel's God has been able to save him.

Verse 20: The king cried out, his voice filled with grief. He called Daniel's God "the living God," just as he had heard Daniel do, and he acknowledged that it is He whom Daniel constantly served. In captivity and at home; in honor and in persecution; in times of prominence and in times of distress, Daniel's faith was constant.

Verse 21: There was no trace of anger in Daniel's reply. He may have known already whose plot it was to destroy him, yet his testimony was immovable.

Verse 22: God has many angelic agencies through whom His will is carried out (Psalm 34:7; 91:11; Heb. 1:14), and through one of these He miraculously shut the lions' mouths. Daniel was not intimating here that he was sinlessly perfect; only that in the matter at hand, he had been obedient to the Lord. He had no intention of being purposely disobedient to King Darius (cf. Matt. 22:21), but rather only appeared so, since his first and highest allegiance was to the Lord.

Verse 23: Although the king had been powerless to reverse his own decree, he was grateful that God had been able to nullify it. Daniel's deliverance was founded upon his faith in God.

Verse 24: Those who dig a pit for others usually manage to fall into it themselves. In this case, although God had delivered Daniel, there was no deliverance for those who had plotted his death. The king now understood how far their jealous conspiracy had spread, even involving the monarch himself. Thus, he rightly responded by inflicting on the guilty the punishment they had intended for the innocent.

When we read that his punishment extended even to their wives and children, it seems unbearably cruel to us; however, in those days that was considered justice and was customary.

Verse 25: Just as King Nebuchadnezzar had written to all peoples and nations of the earth "to declare the signs and wonders which the Most High God has done" (Dan. 4:2), so now King Darius did the same.

Verse 26: It is not certain that Darius sought the sole worship of the true God, but certainly he did desire that the God of Daniel be recognized as a God of power, worthy of reverence. This is the living God, forever the same. And when Darius mentioned that "His dominion will be forever," he revealed a remarkable truth regarding the course of future history: the rule and Kingdom of God shall outlast all Gentile rule on earth, and indeed shall be everlasting.

Verse 27: God is able to rescue, as He has shown in Daniel's case. He is able to work deeds which are beyond the realm of natural possibility.

Verse 28: Again we see that the servant of the Lord did not suffer because of his faithfulness to God. Daniel was restored to his original position of honor and continued to serve both Darius and his nephew and successor, Cyrus the Persian.

Summary of Daniel 1-6: The Dreams of Gentile Rulers

Several spiritual truths are underlined in this familiar yet important portion of Scripture. The calamitous results of envy are sketched clearly, and jealousy is shown to work like a cancer, eating at the very vitals of life. These passages also reveal how blessed it is for a righteous man to be innocent of any accusation. The only course of action open to any potential enemy of the man of God is to accuse him on the very ground of his loyalty to the living God.

In this situation, the Word of God clearly directs our actions. Whenever earthly authorities compete for our allegiance, the Lord God is to come first, always and without exception. Darius's case is a vivid picture of how snares can be laid for a hasty man when one appeals to his pride.

Chapter 6 is unequivocal in its lesson that the condemnation of the law is inescapable (cf. Rom. 6:23). Remember, the law can only accuse; our human consciences can accuse or excuse; yet only God can justify. We are taught in these passages that in their hour of persecution, the righteous may look to God for protection and favor. God can overrule the plans of the enemies of the truth, that ultimately they may be forced to acknowledge His power and strength— though He does not always choose to do so.

With the completion of chapter 6, the fourfold picture of the conduct of world monarchs during the "times of the Gentiles" is now complete. Did these kings rule for God? The answer could not be clearer, and it is no. They advocated and promoted idolatry, as we have seen, by exalting themselves above Almighty God. They became deranged and acted like beasts, until they finally acknowledged the power of God to rule and overrule. They committed the ultimate impiety by profaning the holy things of God, and they set themselves up in the place of God so as to rule out any homage to Him. In each of these cases, there remained only the righteous wrath of God.

In these first six chapters of the book of Daniel, then, the picture is one of unrelieved failure on earth. There is only One worthy to rule on earth, the blessed Son of God, the Lord Jesus Christ. It is He who shall rule on earth some day, as King of kings and Lord of lords. And what a contrast that will be to the picture presented in these first six chapters of the book of Daniel. It is no wonder that the "times of the Gentiles" must be ended and their rule displaced by that of our Lord Jesus Christ.

7 The World Empires and the Little Horn

In the first year of Belshazzar king of Babylon Daniel saw a dream and visions in his mind *as he lay* on his bed; then he wrote the dream down *and* related the following summary of it. ² Daniel said, "I was looking in my vision by night, and behold, the four winds of heaven were stirring up the great sea. ³ And four great beasts were coming up from the sea, different from one another. ⁴ The first *was* like a lion and had *the* wings of an eagle. I kept looking until its wings were plucked, and it was lifted up from the ground and made to stand on two feet like a man; a human mind also was given to it. ⁵ And behold, another beast, a second one, resembling a bear. And it was raised up on one side, and three ribs *were* in its mouth between its teeth; and thus they said to it, 'Arise, devour much meat!' ⁶ After this I kept looking, and behold, another one, like a leopard, which had on its back four wings of a bird; the beast also had four heads, and dominion was given to it. ⁷ After this I kept looking in the night visions, and behold, a fourth beast, dreadful and terrifying and extremely strong; and it had large iron teeth. It devoured and crushed, and trampled down the remainder with its feet; and it was different from all the beasts that were before it, and it had ten horns. ⁸ While I was contemplating the horns, behold, another horn, a little one, came up among them, and three of the first horns were pulled out by the roots before it; and behold, this horn possessed eyes like the eyes of a man, and a mouth uttering great *boasts.*

⁹ "I kept looking
Until thrones were set up,
And the Ancient of Days took *His* seat;
His vesture *was* like white snow,
And the hair of His head like pure wool.

His throne *was* ablaze with flames,
Its wheels *were* a burning fire.

¹⁰ A river of fire was flowing
And coming out from before Him;
Thousands upon thousands were attending Him,
And myriads upon myriads were standing before Him;
The court sat,
And the books were opened.

¹¹ Then I kept looking because of the sound of the boastful words which the horn was speaking; I kept looking until the beast was slain, and its body was destroyed and given to the burning fire. ¹² As for the rest of the beasts, their dominion was taken away, but an extension of life was granted to them for an appointed period of time.

¹³ "I kept looking in the night visions,
And behold, with the clouds of heaven
One like a Son of Man was coming,
And He came up to the Ancient of Days
And was presented before Him.

¹⁴ And to Him was given dominion,
Glory and a kingdom,
That all the peoples, nations, and *men of every*
language
Might serve Him.
His dominion is an everlasting dominion
Which will not pass away;
And His kingdom is one
Which will not be destroyed.

¹⁵ As for me, Daniel, my spirit was distressed within me, and the visions in my mind kept alarming me. ¹⁶ I approached one of those who were standing by and began asking him the exact meaning of all this. So he told me and made known to me the interpretation of these things: ¹⁷ 'These great beasts, which are four *in number*, are four kings *who* will arise from the earth. ¹⁸ But the saints of the Highest One will receive the kingdom and possess the kingdom forever, for all ages to come.' ¹⁹ Then I desired to know the exact meaning of the fourth beast, which was different from all the others, exceedingly dreadful, with its teeth of iron and its claws of

bronze, *and which* devoured, crushed, and trampled down the remainder with its feet, [20] and *the meaning* of the ten horns that *were* on its head, and the other *horn* which came up, and before which three *of them* fell, namely, that horn which had eyes and a mouth uttering great *boasts,* and which was larger in appearance than its associates. [21] I kept looking, and that horn was waging war with the saints and overpowering them [22] until the Ancient of Days came, and judgment was passed in favor of the saints of the Highest One, and the time arrived when the saints took possession of the kingdom.

[23] "Thus he said: 'The fourth beast will be a fourth kingdom on the earth, which will be different from all the *other* kingdoms, and it will devour the whole earth and tread it down and crush it. [24] As for the ten horns, out of this kingdom ten kings will arise; and another will arise after them, and he will be different from the previous ones and will subdue three kings. [25] And he will speak out against the Most High and wear down the saints of the Highest One, and he will intend to make alterations in times and in law; and they will be given into his hand for a time, times, and half a time. [26] But the court will sit *for judgment,* and his dominion will be taken away, annihilated and destroyed forever. [27] Then the sovereignty, the dominion, and the greatness of *all* the kingdoms under the whole heaven will be given to the people of the saints of the Highest One; His kingdom *will be* an everlasting kingdom, and all the dominions will serve and obey Him.' [28] At this point the revelation ended. As for me, Daniel, my thoughts were greatly alarming me and my face grew pale, but I kept the matter to myself."

Introduction

In general, chapter 7 deals with the same theme as chapter 2, but it would be a mistake to think that this is mere repetition. In chapter 2, the four earthly kingdoms and Christ's heavenly kingdom were seen in their outward political appearance; by contrast, chapter 7 presents God's estimate of their innermost moral and spiritual features.

In chapter 2, the symbols were taken from inanimate objects; here in chapter 7, they are taken from the animate. In chapter 2, King Nebuchadnezzar saw the splendor of world empires portrayed in the dazzling statue of a man, while the Kingdom of God was symbolized by a stone. By contrast, in chapter 7, Daniel's vision reveals the animalistic character of world empires and the fact that it is only in the Kingdom of God that man's full dignity is realized—in the Son of Man.

Although beasts can excel man in brute strength, they are far beneath man in moral and spiritual powers. Yet without God, man comes to hopeless ruin and always sinks to the level of bestiality. The lower animals keep their eyes cast down to the ground, unaware of the presence and claims of God above. However, with his erect position and head lifted toward heaven, man shows the lofty destiny God has purposed for the human race.

Verse 1: The events of chapters 7 and 8 properly follow those of chapter 4. This is because here in chapter 7, the events occur "in the first year of Belshazzar," whereas the events of chapter 5 occurred in the last year of his reign (5:30). Since Belshazzar was the last king of Babylon, it was fitting that this second vision of the downfall of world empires should come during his reign.

Daniel had a dream and visions. These were not confused, jumbled-up dreams, but they had distinct images and messages. Daniel wrote his visions down immediately without waiting first for their fulfillment, for he knew that God knows the end from the beginning, the last from the first. Statements such as this offer the strongest possible evidence of the inspiration of God's prophets. In the verses to follow, Daniel recorded the following summary of his visions without going into elaborate detail regarding names, dates, and places.

Verse 2: Daniel saw four great beasts, four representing the four quadrants of the compass. He saw the four winds of heaven stirring the Great Sea, four again symbolizing the universality of these portents. The winds rushed forth, and there was a great commotion among the nations. The study of history teaches that world powers frequently arise from the agitation and disturbance of the established order (Jer. 46:7-8; Luke 21:25; Rev. 13:1; 17:15). On the other hand, the Son of Man and His Kingdom are said to come on the clouds of heaven, which indicates a heavenly, divine origin.

Verse 2 also describes the "Great Sea's" being stirred up. Ordinary Hebrew usage would lead us to identify this as the Mediterranean Sea. Even in Hebrew today, the Mediterranean is referred to as the Great Sea or the Middle Sea. The significance of this reference is that the kingdoms and events soon to be described will center on the Mediterranean region.

Verse 3: Daniel saw four great beasts rise up from the sea, one after the other. The succession of these four great kingdoms was the result of the commotion among the nations, referred to above.

In the Bible, prophets use animals to represent kingdoms and nations. For example, in Ezekiel 29:3-5 the dragon of the Nile represents Egypt and Pharaoh. Again, in Ezekiel 32:2 Pharaoh is compared to a young lion and a whale in the seas. Finally, in Psalm 74:13-14 Egypt is compared to the dragon and leviathan. In the ancient world generally, animals were used as symbols of kingdoms; and even today, the lion represents Great Britain and the eagle the United States.

Notice in this verse that each of the four beasts was different from the other three. Although they all rose from the same watery abyss, each had its own distinctive features.

Verse 4: The first beast is now described. It was like a lion and had eagle's wings—although they were plucked. The beast was lifted up so that it stood upright like a man, and it was given the heart, or mind, of a man as well.

The lion is the king of beasts, noted for its strength and majesty (Gen. 49:9). The king represented by this beast would be enormously powerful, keeping all the nations in submission to himself. However, a lion is ordinarily not thought of as being particularly swift in his movements; to convey the swiftness of this first king, the wings of an eagle were added.

If eagle wings symbolized swiftness, the clipping of those wings conveyed the idea of some hindrance that impeded the eagle's normally swift progress. His power and conquests somehow were checked. The fact that this first beast was portrayed in an unnatural, upright posture was intended to convey that the lion's natural strength and ferocity had been reduced to the comparative weakness of a man. The fact that the lion was given the mind, or heart, of a man means that the lion was given the nature and disposition of a man. The initial ferocity of this kingdom would be completely transformed into humane moderation. Compare this with 4:16 and 4:34-36, where this process was reversed.

The lion unquestionably symbolized the Babylonian Empire, thus corresponding to the statue's head of gold in chapter 2. It was leonine in its initial conquests, and the rapidity of its successes was well symbolized by eagle wings. The fact that those wings were clipped referred to the way in which King Nebuchadnezzar's successors were unable to continue his conquests. They were weak leaders who gradually weakened and caused the eventual decline of the empire Nebuchadnezzar had begun. By contrast, recall that Nebuchadnezzar had learned the lessons of God and that his mind and strength were consequently restored to him (4:34-37).

Verse 5: The second beast Daniel saw in his vision was a bear. The bear is known for his cunning and rapacity (2 Sam. 17:8; Hos. 13:8), his roughness, and his savagery and cruelty to his enemies. The bear, this verse says, "was raised up on one side." The kingdom that had heretofore been at rest was now rousing itself for brutal conquest. This refers to the coalition government of the Medo-Persian Empire, which was composed of the more passive Medes and the more aggressive Persians.

We read further that "three ribs were in its mouth between its teeth." Some believe that this referred to three cities that were brought under Persian domination; others suggest it referred to parts of the kingdom. It is futile to speculate on which specific geographical area was meant, but just as each beast referred to an empire, so the parts of each animal referred to the parts of an empire. Beyond this basic understanding it is unnecessary to go.

Finally, the word came to this second beast, "Arise, devour much meat!" God had granted this second kingdom the authority to subjugate many nations, all in keeping with the greedy nature of bears.

Verse 6: The third beast that appeared in Daniel's vision was a leopard. This animal is known for his bloodthirstiness, cruelty, and swiftness (Hab. 1:8). This beast symbolized the small Greek kingdom of Macedon, whose king, Alexander the Great, attacked the enormous Persian Empire that extended from the Aegean Sea to the Indus River. In twelve short years, Alexander conquered part of Europe and all of Asia from the Adriatic to the Indus.

Whereas the symbol of Babylon had but two wings, this beast was seen to have four. It was to be characterized by even greater swiftness than those that had preceded it. Alexander knew the principles of what today would be called the *blitzkrieg,* and he employed them in his campaigns of conquest.

We read further that this leopard had four heads. When Alexander the Great died in 323 B.C., his kingdom was divided among his four generals—Ptolemy, Seleucus, Lysimachus, and Cassander—who then became the four "heads" of the Hellenistic Empire. Dominion was given to this empire not by Alexander or any other mortal, but by God Himself. No other explanation can account for the fact that Alexander's thirty thousand man army was able to conquer Persian armies of several hundreds of thousands. **Verse 7:** Daniel next described the fourth beast he saw in his vision. Although this was part of the dream that occupies this entire chapter, it is set apart from the other portions in an emphatic way. The first three beasts were a lion, a bear, and a leopard, but this fourth beast was unnamed. It was so terrible as to be beyond description.

The distinguishing mark of this beast was its ability to break and stamp all it met. Its destructive power was underscored by the references to its "iron teeth" and its crushing feet. Whatever this beast could not devour with its iron teeth, it crushed and stamped with its feet. The image we are given here is one of unrelieved power and fury.

This fourth beast had ten horns. In prophetic literature, a horn is a symbol of power, since animals use their horns as weapons of destruction. In this case, the ten horns represented ten powerful kings, as explained in verse 24, and corresponded to the ten toes of the statue that were described in 2:40-42.

Verse 8: At this point, for the first time in this vision, a change occurred in the objects Daniel saw. The first three beasts had passed away in the very same form they had appeared, but Daniel witnessed a change in the appearance of the fourth.

Among the ten horns of this fourth beast there arose another little horn, which "pulled out by the roots" three of the other horns. According to this verse, the little horn "possessed eyes like the eyes of a man," which symbolizes intelligence (Ezek. 1:18). This meant that the fourth great world power will be noted for its wisdom and natural intelligence. It will devise its plans shrewdly and execute them well.

Finally, the little horn was described as having "a mouth uttering great boasts," which clearly betrays its haughty arrogance. Later in this chapter, verse 25 informs us that these boasts will include blasphemy and persecution of the saints. The world has certainly heard more than enough blasphemy during its long history; yet the greatest blasphemy of all still remains to be committed during the Tribulation, when the church is gone to glory.

Verse 9: Daniel continued to ponder the strange sight of the four beasts "until thrones were set up" for the administration of justice. Having just described the fourth beast in the preceding verse, we now are told of the judgment that awaits him.

Notice here that more than one throne is to be set up. The Lord Jesus Christ will sit as Judge (John 5:26-27), but the church shall also judge the world and angels (1 Cor. 6:2-3). These events revolving around the fourth beast are preparatory to the reign of the saints with Christ in His earthly kingdom, for the solemn seat of judgment must be set up before that reign can begin.

The "Ancient of Days" was seated for the purpose of passing sentence. This term refers to His great age and is a way of expressing the majesty of the Judge, the Eternal One (Psalm 90:2). His white garment is symbolic of purity and honor, thus assuring that His judgment will be just. His hair, "like pure wool," speaks of His having attained an age of mature judgment. His throne was "ablaze with flames." Fire is used in Scripture as a symbol of judgment and punishment, as well as of the chastening righteousness of God.

Verse 10: There is "a river of fire" flowing out before Him from that throne of judgment, as everything is pervaded by the wonderful holiness of God. There are multitudes ministering to Him, and innumerable myriads of witnesses are present as sentence is pronounced. God's judgment is ever according to truth, so the records of the deeds of the one to be judged will be open for all to see. The bill of particulars for the accused will be drawn up, and the brief will be in proper order.

Verse 11: Because of the diabolical ways and the blasphemous boasting of the little horn, the judgment that is pronounced against him in heaven will be executed on earth. The destruction of the beast's body can only mean that the empire he represents will be destroyed. The burning of his body is in keeping with the doctrine of God's final retribution, from which there is no escape:

> And the beast was seized, and with him the false
> prophet who performed the signs in his presence...
> these two were thrown alive into the lake of fire
> which burns with brimstone [Rev. 19:20].

Verse 12: The difference between the first three kingdoms and the last is clearly brought out in this verse. The first three ceased to rule as kingdoms because their power was taken from them; however, they were still allowed to exist "for an appointed period of time." Their dominion was superseded by that of other empires, but their natural life continued.

Verse 13: As Daniel continued to look, he saw "one like a Son of Man." What does this expression mean? To whom does it refer? The expression "Son of Man" does refer to one who is a man, but it has some added emphasis as well. It is used often in the prophecy of Ezekiel to refer to the prophet's frailty and humanity. The root meaning for the word *man* is "weakness" and "feebleness." In the New Testament, the expression was used only by Christ of Himself, to show that He is truly one of us, in every essential respect a man. It relates Christ to the promise of the Redeemer as the seed of woman, a part of the human race (Gen. 3:15). But there is more than mere humanity in view in this passage, for He is promised universal dominion, and God never shares eternal power and rule with man.

Early Jewish and Christian interpreters understood this

One to be the Messiah, a position the New Testament abundantly confirms (see, e.g., Matt. 16:28; 19:28; 24:27, 30, 39, 44; 25:31, 34). In this passage, the judgment has already taken place on earth in fulfillment of the Lord's prayer: "Thy kingdom come. Thy will be done, on earth as it is in heaven" (Matt. 6:10). Throughout the Scriptures, the title "Son of Man" refers to Christ's coming again for His kingdom. He receives honor and glory from the Ancient of Days because He is the Savior and Redeemer of the lost, having forfeited heaven when Adam listened to Satan instead of God. Now, just as Christ used this name in the days of His humiliation, He will again claim it in the days of His majesty as Lord

When the "Son of Man" comes to the Ancient of Days, it is to be invested with the authority of the kingdom (Psalm 110:1-2). Ever since His death on Calvary, the kingdom has been Christ's by title and by actual exercise. At His second coming, He will actually, visibly administer this kingdom. That will be the hour of reckoning—when He will deal with those who have been delegated some power over this kingdom during the times of the Gentiles, but who have misused it for their own glory. You may be sure that the rightful King will not allow His commitment to be mismanaged endlessly; He will call the responsible parties to account.

Verse 14: In unmistakable terms, this verse teaches that universal rule and sovereignty are bestowed upon Messiah by the consent and authority of the Ancient of Days. This reign will be as far-reaching as are the benefits of Christ's wonderful sacrifice on Calvary, which was for all men of all ages, and which can be received by any trusting heart.

The latter portion of this verse is significant, for although the first half could possibly describe the rule of some of the human empires described in this book, this second half refers to the new kingdom in terms that can only be true of the Messiah of God, the Lord Jesus Christ. His kingdom will never pass away, nor can it ever suffer destruction. No power in heaven, on earth, or under the earth can ever bring it to an end. All nations will "serve" Him: the word here translated "serve" may more fully be rendered as "divine service and worship." This is yet another proof that the Son of Man is truly and absolutely God.

Verse 15: Daniel was troubled in spirit by what he saw. On the one hand, he understood enough to know that this vision spoke of dismal failure on the part of human rulers; yet there were also other features that led him to hope for further light.

Verse 16: In order to understand all he had seen, Daniel approached one of the attendants already mentioned in verse 10. He was not disappointed, for the angel explained the meaning of the vision to the prophet, who has passed these revealed truths on to us.

Verse 17: Kingdoms are often represented by their rulers; thus, kings and kingdoms are sometimes used interchangeably (cf. 8:21). Each of the four kings represented an empire on earth. Particular attention should be given to the fact that "the earth" is mentioned, for in verse 3 we saw that the symbols of nations arose from the sea. Here, however, explicit mention of the earth indicates that these predicted empires would be actual kingdoms on earth, holding sway over the nations.

Verse 18: For the first time, reference is made to the "saints of the Highest One." This verse reveals that when the Son of Man takes the reins of government into His blessed hands, He will not rule alone. The godly Israelites who have waited and longed for Messiah's kingdom—Abraham, Moses, David, Daniel, and so many others—will reign along with Him. In Matthew 19:28 the Lord Jesus revealed to His disciples that they, too, would sit on thrones and judge the twelve tribes of Israel.

Verse 19: The fourth beast remains the most remarkable of them all. Daniel asked no further questions about the first three beasts he saw, but the fourth was so striking, so powerful, so irresistible, that he felt he must know more about it. The little horn was so unusual, the judgment pronounced upon it by the Son of Man so solemn and majestic; what could it all mean?

Verse 20: By its cunning and blasphemy, this little horn will be able to displace three of the other horns and usurp their power and prestige. Then it will feel itself capable of asserting its preeminence over all the other horns, as well.

Verse 21: The little horn of the beast will be allowed to wage war against the saints, as is also described in Revelation 11:7 and 13:7. Although the saints will be powerless to oppose him by their own strength, he will prevail over them only temporarily.

Verse 22: This permission to persecute the saints is granted by the Ancient of Days for a time, until He calls an end to his days. He waits until the little horn's blasphemy has reached its height, and then judgment is passed. Now the tables are turned, and those who had been persecuted are placed in the position of judges over the wicked horn. Their position includes the right to rule, as well (Rev. 20:4).

Verse 23: There can be no doubt about the interpretation of the symbols in this vision when the kingdoms are so clearly singled out.

Verse 24: The ten horns described here correspond to the ten toes of the great statue (2:40-42). In the same general area as that occupied by the ancient Roman Empire, there will arise a confederacy of ten nations, a counterfeit kingdom with a semblance of universal power. This little horn is contemporaneous with the ten others and arises from among them. The Roman beast, ruler of the end time, will arise from the midst of the ten-nation confederacy and command the whole coalition.

Verse 25: His arrogance and self-promotion will know no

bounds. He will oppose both God in heaven and man on earth, both the Lord and His saints. He will seek to make alterations "in times and in law" in order to garner for himself the worship of mankind. That is, he will advocate changing the times of the feast days of Israel, just as Jeroboam had done after the reign of Solomon (1 Kings 12:28-33). This idolater of the end time will try to eradicate the distinctive character of the worship of Israel.

He will be allowed to succeed for a specified length of time. This period is referred to as "a time, times, and half a time." From 4:16 and 23, we learn that "a time" actually means a year; thus the saints will be given into the hand of the little horn for three and one-half years. This is the same 42 months or 1260 days referred to in Revelation 11:2 and 12:6; it is called "the time of Jacob's distress" in Jeremiah 30:7. This is the Great Tribulation, when the beast in Rome and the Antichrist in Jerusalem will form their alliance to dominate religious and political life on earth.

Verse 26: No matter how successful the rule of the fourth beast may appear, it will not be permanent. Divine judgment will intervene, his dominion will end, and his destruction will be final. This verse does not specify by whom the beast's end will come, yet we saw earlier in 2:44 that it is an act of Almighty God. Every power that has been set up against God will be done away with.

Verse 27: All the greatness and prestige the four great world empires longed for will be the portion of Messiah's kingdom on earth. The Messiah has ever a heart for downtrodden people, so when He enters into His reign of glory, they will share the reign with Him. This will be an eternal kingdom, for after its earthly phase has been fulfilled, it will continue in even greater glory and beauty throughout eternity.

Verse 28: These thoughts "greatly alarmed" and troubled Daniel. This reveals that the Holy Spirit had intended much more by Daniel's words than he himself understood at the time. We should never limit the significance of the prophetic Scriptures to only what the prophets themselves understood (cf. 1 Pet. 1:10-12). Daniel hid all these matters in his heart, and we will do well to do the same. God has His plan, and we do well to fit into it.

Summary of chapter 7

This is one of the pivotal chapters in the Bible, as well as in the book of Daniel itself. The great powers of the "times of the Gentiles" (Luke 21:24) were represented in Daniel's vision by the figures of the four great beasts rising from the sea. The sea was tempestuous, agitated by violent winds.

But the wicked are like the
    tossing sea,
For it cannot be quiet,
And its waters toss up refuse
    and mud.
"There is no peace," says my
    God, "for the wicked" [Isa. 57:20-21].

Kingdom after kingdom has arisen on earth, born amid agitation and violence. No matter how illustrious and pompous these kingdoms appear to the outward eye, they are all essentially brutish. Like the beasts of the field, they are more powerful than any individual man, yet their true dignity is far beneath that of man, who was created in the image of Almighty God.

The spiritual union that man can enjoy with God is impossible for any of the lower creatures of the universe. World rulers whose thoughts and actions separate them from God are reduced to the level of beasts of blind passion. That which ennobles man is utter, willing surrender to the living God. When man tries to be independent of God, he does not lift himself up, but rather plunges himself into the pit. It is spiritual catastrophe, and it is the suicide of the soul.

The first great kingdom, Babylon, is seen in this chapter to have been restored to a position of dignity and worth by being first abased and clothed with humility. With reference to the second and third kingdoms, this chapter has shown that all their greedy conquests were kept strictly within rigid limits by the restraining hand of God. This should always be a source of comfort to the saints of God; He will not allow them to do lasting harm to His own.

No known beast can represent the fourth kingdom, because it is such a horrible combination of so many dreadful features of the previous powers (cf. Rev. 13:1). It is in the last ruler of this kingdom, who will obtain his position by ruthless usurpations, by remarkable intellectual powers and by unheard-of blasphemies, that all God-defying principles will find their final culmination. The seasons of the holy festivals, which were established by the Lord God, will not be left in their proper places by this wicked ruler. All must conform to these new outrages, just as was the order of the day in Nebuchadnezzar's time.

But all that transpires on earth is under the clear eye of God, so when the proper hour arrives, God will sit in judgment on this fourth kingdom. Rule will be quickly stripped from it, and swift destruction will follow, for which there is no remedy. The Lord Jesus Christ will then take over government of the earth and will permit His kingdom to be administered by the saints of the Most High.

8 The Vision of the Ram and the Goat

In the third year of the reign of Belshazzar the king a vision appeared to me, Daniel, subsequent to the one which appeared to me previously. ² And I looked in the vision, and it came about while I was looking, that I was in the citadel of Susa, which is in the province of Elam; and I looked in the vision, and I myself was beside the Ulai Canal. ³ Then I lifted my gaze and looked, and behold, a ram which had two horns was standing in front of the canal. Now the two horns *were* long, but one *was* longer than the other, with the longer one coming up last. ⁴ I saw the ram butting westward, northward, and southward, and no *other* beasts could stand before him, nor was there anyone to rescue from his power; but he did as he pleased and magnified *himself*. ⁵ While I was observing, behold, a male goat was coming from the west over the surface of the whole earth without touching the ground; and the goat *had* a conspicuous horn between his eyes. ⁶ And he came up to the ram that had the two horns, which I had seen standing in front of the canal, and rushed at him in his mighty wrath. And I saw him come beside the ram, and he was enraged at him; and he struck the ram and shattered his two horns, and the ram had no strength to withstand him. So he hurled him to the ground and trampled on him, and there was none to rescue the ram from his power. ⁸ Then the male goat magnified *himself* exceedingly. But as soon as he was mighty, the large horn was broken; and in its place there came up four conspicuous *horns* toward the four winds of heaven.

⁹ And out of one of them came forth a rather small horn which grew exceedingly great toward the south, toward the east, and toward the Beautiful *Land*. ¹⁰ And it grew up to the host of heaven and caused some of the host and some of the stars to fall to the

earth, and it trampled them down. [11] It even magnified *itself* to be equal with the Commander of the host; and it removed the regular sacrifice from Him, and the place of His sanctuary was thrown down. [12] And on account of transgression the host will be given over *to the horn* along with the regular sacrifice; and it will fling truth to the ground and perform *its will* and prosper. [13] Then I heard a holy one speaking, and another holy one said to that particular one who was speaking, "How long will the vision *about* the regular sacrifice apply, while the transgression causes horror, so as to allow both the holy place and the host to be trampled?" [14] And he said to me, "For 2,300 evenings *and* mornings; then the holy place will be properly restored."

[15] And it came about when I, Daniel, had seen the vision, that I sought to understand it; and behold, standing before me was one who looked like a man. [16] And I heard the voice of a man between *the banks of* Ulai, and he called out and said, "Gabriel, give this *man* an understanding of the vision." [17] So he came near to where I was standing, and when he came I was frightened and fell on my face; but he said to me, "Son of man, understand that the vision pertains to the time of the end." [18] Now while he was talking with me, I sank into a deep sleep with my face to the ground; but he touched me and made me stand upright. [19] And he said, "Behold, I am going to let you know what will occur at the final period of the indignation, for *it* pertains to the appointed time of the end. [20] The ram which you saw with the two horns represents the kings of Media and Persia. [21] And the shaggy goat *represents* the kingdom of Greece, and the large horn that is between his eyes is the first king. [22] And the broken *horn* and the four *horns that* arose in its place *represent* four kingdoms *which* will arise from *his* nation, although not with his power.

[23] And in the latter period of their rule,
  When the transgressors have run *their course,*
  A king will arise
  Insolent and skilled in intrigue.
[24] And his power will be mighty, but not by his *own* power,
  And he will destroy to an extraordinary degree
  And prosper and perform *his will;*
  He will destroy mighty men and the holy people.

²⁵ And through his shrewdness
He will cause deceit to succeed by his influence;
And he will magnify *himself* in his heart,
And he will destroy many while *they are* at ease.
He will even oppose the Prince of princes,
But he will be broken without human agency.
²⁶ And the vision of the evenings and mornings
Which has been told is true;
But keep the vision secret,
For it pertains to many days *in the future.*"
²⁷ Then I, Daniel, was exhausted and sick for days. Then I got up *again* and carried on the king's business; but I was astounded at the vision, and there was none to explain *it*.

Introduction

The first portion of the book of Daniel was written in Hebrew from 1:1 to 2:4, at which point the original language changed to Aramaic. That Gentile language was used to describe events that center on the "times of the Gentiles," which our Lord described in Luke 21.

As chapter 8 begins, however, the visions it contains relate entirely to the Jews and the city of Jerusalem. For that reason, the language of the original text now reverts to Hebrew and remains so throughout the rest of the book of Daniel.

The subject of chapter 8 is somewhat more narrow than what it was in chapters 2 and 7, which described all four of the major world empires. In this chapter, the text confines itself to the second and third empires, the Medo-Persian and the Greek. These are especially interesting to the student of biblical prophecy, for they are among the few prophecies in the Bible that were explained to the prophets who received them. By studying these carefully, they become a valuable guide to illuminate the meaning of other, similar prophecies.

Verse 1: The events of chapter 7 occurred during the first year of the reign of Belshazzar (7:1). The visions described in this chapter were seen two years later, during his third year of rule, and probably came soon before the end of this reign. We read here that the visions he was about to relate appeared to him after the visions he had already described in chapter 7.

Verse 2: Some say that Daniel was at the citadel of Shushan only in spirit, or in a vision, and that certainly is possible. However, it is also possible that he was physically there. The city of Shushan was located in the province of Elam and was comparatively insignificant at that time (cf. Esther 1:2, 5). It was not until later that it became the capital of Persia. Elam was west of Persia proper, east of Babylonia, and south of Media. "The Ulai" mentioned here is the river Eulaeus, also known to later Greek writers as the Choaspes, insofar as we can tell (scholars disagree on the ancient names of many things).

Verse 3: Daniel first saw the ram with two horns. It is impossible to mistake the identity of this animal, because it was explicitly declared in verse 20: "The ram which you saw with the two horns represents the kings of Media and Persia." It referred, then, to the kings of the Medo-Persian Empire, which followed the Babylonian Empire. This was the empire represented by the breast and arms of silver in the vision of the great statue (2:31-32); and by the bear in the vision of the four beasts (7:5).

The horn is still a symbol of power, as it was in chapter 7. One of the ram's horns is longer than the other, with the longer one coming up last. This longer horn represents Persia, which was of little importance until the time of Cyrus. Under his leadership, Persia came to overshadow Media, even though Media was the more ancient kingdom.

From 5:31, we learn that Darius the Mede was sixty-two years old when he began to reign over the Medo-Persian

Empire. During his brief two-year reign, power passed from the hands of this weak king until the government was almost entirely in the hands of Cyrus the Persian. Appropriately, the king of Persia wore a jeweled lamb's head of gold instead of a crown. Finally, this one horn raised higher than the other recalls the bear that was raised up on one side (7:5).

Verse 4: The ram's conquests are now sketched for us. Notice that the east is not mentioned, because none of the conquests of the Medo-Persian Empire extended in that direction. However, to the west they conquered Babylonia, Mesopotamia, Syria, and Asia Minor. To the north they conquered Colchis, Armenia, Iberia, and parts of the coast of the Caspian Sea. Their conquests to the south included Palestine, Ethiopia, Egypt, and Libya. Medo-Persian power itself was seen as coming from the east (cf. Isa. 41:2; 46:11).

According to this verse, the ram "did as he pleased and magnified himself." Nevertheless, it was according to God's own will that the Medo-Persian Empire encountered no successful opposition during its early military campaigns and grew to cover a great part of the known world. Its progress continued unchecked until later, when the Greeks under Alexander the Great subdued it.

Verse 5: Daniel next saw a male goat, which verse 21 identifies as the symbol of the kingdom of Greece. The goat had "a conspicuous horn between his eyes," which verse 21 identifies as its first king. These refer to the Graeco-Macedonian Empire of Alexander the Great, who went forth to conquer the great Persian Empire. This empire used to be symbolized by a goat, as is confirmed by the discovery of bronze figures of a goat that date from that period. So you see, these prophecies could be understood by the people of that day after Daniel had declared them.

This verse also indicates that the male goat "was coming from the west over the surface of the whole earth." He seemed to reach out over the whole world. This well describes the movements of Alexander, who conquered the entire known world—and then wept because there were no more worlds to conquer! This male goat moved so swiftly, it was said that he moved "without touching the ground." This denoted the amazing rapidity of his conquests. Alexander had been chosen commander of the Greek forces against the Persians at the age of twenty-one, and by the time he died twelve years later at the age of thirty-three, he had brought the entire known world to his feet. His victories were more rapid and more decisive than any that had come before him. This verse refers to Alexander as the "conspicuous horn," as if all the power of Greece were concentrated in him.

Verse 6: Daniel saw the male goat rush at the ram "in his mighty wrath." This referred to the fierceness with which Alexander struck out at the Persian Empire. Notice, too, that he rushed at the ram "in front of the canal," or river. It was at the river Granicus that Alexander fought his first victorious battle against Darius the Mede, in 334 B.C. And from the Battle of Granicus to the Battle of Arbela only three years elapsed, during which the entire Persian Empire fell apart.

Verse 7: Alexander the Great represented all the concentrated wrath that the Greeks directed against the Persians because of the Persian invasion of Greece more than a century before. In 331 B.C., Alexander defeated Darius Codomannus, and when he burned Persepolis (Greek for "city of Persia") the next year, the conquest of Persia was complete. All the great hosts of the Persian Empire were insufficient to save her from Alexander's small army.

Verse 8: As soon as this male goat that Daniel saw became mighty, we read that "the large horn was broken." The Hellenistic Empire of Alexander the Great had reached its greatest strength and extent, occupying the entire known world, when suddenly Alexander died in 323 B.C. The empire never recovered from the shock of his loss and never regained the strength it possessed under his leadership.

We read further in this verse that in the place of the broken large horn, "there came up four conspicuous horns toward the four winds of heaven." Upon the death of Alexander, a long and confused power struggle erupted among his generals. The Hellenistic Empire was finally divided among the four victorious generals, each of whom ruled over a quarter of the empire. Seleucus assumed power over the eastern portion of the empire, Cassander over the west, Ptolemy over the south, and Lysimachus over the north. This fourfold division explains the reference in this verse to "the four winds of heaven," and each of those generals was represented by one of the four horns.

Verse 9: The "small horn" referred to here has been taken by some to mean the "little horn" described in chapter 7. However, if one compares the two passages carefully, it is clear that they do not refer to the same things at all. In chapter 7, the "little horn" arose from the fourth world empire, whereas this "small horn" arises from the third. In chapter 7, the "little horn" arose as an eleventh horn following the first ten, whereas here the "small horn" comes out of the four horns of the male goat. Thus the two cannot be taken to refer to the same thing.

This "rather small horn...grew exceedingly great." It is generally agreed that this horn represented Antiochus Epiphanes of Syria, who reigned there in the second century B.C. In fact, one of the ancient translations of the Old Testament—the Syriac version—inserts into the text of the Bible here the words "Antiochus Epiphanes." Antiochus, whose name meant "illustrious one," was the eighth king of the dynasty founded in Syria by Alexander's general Seleucus. The noncanonical book of First Maccabees, which was written during the time between the Old and New Testaments, describes Antiochus in the following way:

So Alexander died after a reign of twelve years. His

officers then took power, each in his own territory. They all assumed royal diadems after his death, and their descendants continued to succeed them for many years and brought much evil upon the world. A wicked shoot sprouted from this stock, Antiochus Epiphanes, son of King Antiochus. This Antiochus Epiphanes, after having been a hostage in Rome, became king in the year 137 of the Hellenistic dynasty [1 Maccabees 1:7-10].

Continuing in verse 9, we read that this "small horn" grew "toward the south, toward the east, and toward the Beautiful Land." This referred to the conquests of Antiochus after he assumed power. He grew "toward the south" when he conquered Egypt in 170 B.C.; "toward the east" when he assumed rule over the former territories of the Persian Empire; and finally "toward the Beautiful Land" of Palestine (cf. Psalm 48:2; 50:2). When Antiochus Epiphanes returned from his Egyptian campaign, he invaded Judea, captured Jerusalem, robbed the Temple, and spread his reign of terror across the land.

Verse 10: As his successful campaigns continued, Antiochus's power continued to grow until "it grew up to the host of heaven." Some have understood this passage to mean that in his madness, Antiochus sought to exalt himself above the stars (cf. Isa. 14:12-14). Instead, it is better to understand that Antiochus made war on the holy army of the Lord, that is, the priests and worshipers of the Lord God.

Such was Antiochus's pride that nothing was beyond the bounds of his ambition. He even "caused some of the host and some of the stars to fall to the earth." The history of those times reveals that Antiochus succeeded only too well in his diabolical designs on the people of God. In Jerusalem, he sought to substitute the Greek god Zeus for the Lord God. He also introduced sacrifices to idols in the Temple. Antiochus further sought to blot out the distinctive character of Jewish culture by encouraging Jews to adopt Greek customs. Finally, he profaned the Sabbath and the Temple of the holy covenant. In all these ways, Antiochus Epiphanes ran roughshod over the customs and sensibilities of the people of God and, in the words of this verse, he "trampled them down." This reveals the utter contempt he had for all the Jews held dear, and it serves as a striking summary of how he fulfilled the prophecies in this passage.

Verse 11: When a man's blasphemy is allowed to go unchecked, his wicked heart is encouraged to carry his designs even further. In this case, it was not enough that Antiochus conducted himself toward God's people in the way he did; he felt ready to array himself even against God.

Some interpret the "Commander of the host" as a reference to the Jewish high priest who lived during Antiochus's reign; it is more probable, however, that it referred to the Lord Himself. Thus, the *New American Standard Bible* capitalizes "Commander" to signify His identity.

It was evident that by his every act, Antiochus Epiphanes sought to displace God's laws with his own and to supplant the worship of the true God with idolatry of the gods of the Greek pantheon. Here in this verse was yet another attempt on the part of this blasphemer to impose uniformity at any price. He removed the "regular sacrifice" that daily offered up a lamb in the morning and the evening. This sacrifice had been explicitly commanded by the Lord God (cf. Exod. 29:38-39), yet it was now forbidden by this godless usurper. Once again the noncanonical book of First Maccabees provides the history of this desecration:

> The king [Antiochus] wrote to all his kingdom, for all to become one people and for each to abandon his own customs. All the Gentiles agreed to the terms of the king's proclamation. Many Israelites, too, accepted his religion and sacrificed to idols and violated the Sabbath. The king sent letters by messengers to Jeru-

salem and the towns of Judah containing orders to follow customs foreign to the land, to put a stop to burnt offerings and meal offering and libation in the temple, to violate Sabbaths and festivals, to defile temple and holy things, to build illicit altars and illicit temples and idolatrous shrines, to sacrifice swine and ritually unfit animals, to leave their sons uncircumcised, and to draw abomination upon themselves by means of all kinds of uncleanness and profanation, so as to forget the Torah [the Law of Moses] and violate all the commandments. Whoever disobeyed the word of the king was to be put to death [1 Maccabees 1:44-50].

Finally, we read in verse eleven that "the place of His sanctuary was thrown down." Although Antiochus did not literally destroy God's holy Temple, he robbed, plundered, and removed its holy vessels, so that its services were discontinued.

Verse 12: We read here that "on account of transgression the host will be given over to the horn." The "host" referred to here are the people of Israel, just as in verse 10.

There were some Jewish apostates who made Antiochus's work easier for him by their transgressions against the Law of God. Impiety was prevalent in Israel in those days, and in a sense Antiochus's vile acts were a visitation of the Lord's judgment for their sins. Even the noncanonical book of First Maccabees traces these calamities to the deeds of wicked men who worked with Antiochus to introduce heathen practices into Israel (1 Maccabees 1:43).

This verse goes on to say that the horn would "fling truth to the ground." The true worship and knowledge of God was trampled underfoot by Antiochus, and, strangely enough, he continued to prosper. His plan against Jerusalem was permitted to succeed because God was using him to purge Israel of those who merely professed to know Him, "holding to a form of godliness, although they have denied its power" (2 Tim. 3:5).

Verse 13: With the end of this vision, Daniel next overheard one angel speaking to another, asking how long this desolation was to continue. Again, the desolation here referred both to the desecration of the Temple and the oppression of God's people.

Verse 14: Why did the answer to the angel's question come to Daniel? Because it was for his comfort and the comfort of God's people throughout the ages. In language strongly reminiscent of Genesis 1, the desolation was to last "for 2,300 evenings and mornings" and was to end with the cleansing of the Temple. Antiochus began his oppression of the Jews in 171 B.C.; and it was 2,300 days later, in December of 165 B.C., that it ended with the cleansing of the Temple by Judas Maccabaeus.

Failure to understand the exact nature of this prophecy has led many to blunder into even more grave errors that touch the very heart of our faith. It was from the misinterpretation of this verse that the whole system of Seventh Day Adventism arose. It must be stressed that these 2,300 days have already run their course in the history of the Jews; nothing is said here about a future people or a future period of time.

As we said, in 165 B.C. Judas Maccabaeus fulfilled this prophecy by cleansing the defiled sanctuary. He designated a new priesthood to minister in the Temple, and he pulled down the defiling heathen altar that had been erected there. He carried out all the defiled stones to an unclean place and built a new altar in place of the old one Antiochus had defiled. He repaired the courts; replaced the altar of incense, the table of the bread of the Presence, and the golden lampstands; and he rededicated them all to the sole service of God. This rededication occurred on the twenty-fifth day of Chislev and was celebrated for eight days. It was known as the Feast of Lights, or Feast of Dedication, and is still celebrated annually by the Jews as Chanukah, which means "dedication" (cf. John 10:22).

Verse 15: Daniel had seen a vision, but he was unable to understand it. While he struggled to comprehend the meaning of what he had seen, "one who looked like a man" stood before him. This was the angel Gabriel in human form (cf. Luke 1:19).

Verse 16: The voice of God commanded Gabriel to make known to Daniel the meaning of the vision. The name Gabriel means "man of God," or "strong man of God," and is mentioned only in Daniel 8:16; 9:21; and in Luke 1:19, 26, where Gabriel announced to Mary the coming of her virgin-born Son.

Verse 17: When Daniel saw the angelic messenger, he was completely overpowered and fell on his face. Gabriel encouraged him to understand that he had been shown a vision of "the time of the end." This expression is a very important one throughout Scripture, referring to the series of events that will end in the establishment of the kingdom of the Lord Jesus Christ. In this case, Daniel was encouraged to look beyond the evil times of Antiochus Epiphanes and take comfort in the triumph of the righteous that is to come.

Verse 18: When the prophet was overcome by the vision, he sank senseless to the ground. But Gabriel touched Daniel at once, strengthened him, and set him on his feet.

Verse 19: When all the scriptural passages that refer to the "final period of the indignation" are compared, it will be seen that they refer very specifically to a future trial of God's beloved people, Israel (cf. Jer. 30:1-7).

It is thus clear that just as the fourth kingdom in chapter 7 will play a distinct role in the end time, so the third kingdom will as well. Such views used to be the object of much ridicule in years gone by, but in recent years the nations of that part of the world have undergone a tremendous revival. Today we see that the events predicted in this chapter could easily come to pass. For that reason, we must be careful not to restrict the meaning of these prophecies solely to the times of Antiochus Epiphanes. The 2,300 days of the desolation referred to Antiochus, but also to other matters beyond him: what happened in his day was merely a foreshadowing of what will result when Israel enters into the "final period of the indignation."

Verse 20: Since the symbols of this prophecy are so simply and clearly explained, there is no reason for any reader to misunderstand its meaning. The interpretation offered here is not merely the opinion of some mortal man but the infallible word of the Holy Spirit. As a result, this interpretation determines the meaning of the entire chapter and guides our understanding of it.

Verse 21: This is the equally inspired explanation of the second beast. The first king of the Greek kingdom, as we said before, was Alexander the Great; he was the first man ever to consolidate Greek power into a united kingdom when he led his Hellenistic armies against the Persian Empire.

Verse 22: The "broken horn" here refers to Alexander's death at the height of his power and success. We read further that there would be "four kingdoms which will arise from his nation, although not with his power." As was stated earlier, none of the four Hellenistic kingdoms that resulted from Alexander's death was as powerful as his had been.

Verse 23: Just as the Roman Empire will be revived during the last days, so, too, the lands that were the scene of Greek domination will reenter the center stage of world history. The events described here cannot refer to the times of Antiochus Epiphanes, for too many details given here were not fulfilled during his reign.

The testimony of Scripture is that in the days just before the visible reign of the Lord Jesus Christ, there will be three main powers competing with each other, all of which will be opposed to the will of God. First, the beast of Rome will establish the revived Roman Empire in southern Europe; he is primarily a political figure. Second, the Antichrist will concentrate his activity in Israel and will sit in the Temple of God; he is primarily a religious figure. And third, a ruler of the north will arise from the land of the former Greek Empire; he is primarily a military figure. Some have identified the king of the north with the Antichrist, but the two arise from different parts of the world. Although they do appear on the scene during the same historical period, they are of different nationalities and are opposed to each other.

How can we be certain that this passage could not refer to the days of Antiochus Epiphanes? The answer lies in this verse, where we read that these events will occur "when the transgressors have run their course." That could also be translated "when the transgressions have come to the full." Surely transgressions have multiplied since the days of Antiochus Epiphanes; this passage must thus refer to a future, culminating age when all transgression will have run its course.

God will not allow evil to go unpunished. The Scriptures tell consistently that these conditions will immediately precede Christ's visible return to earth to establish His righteous kingdom in Jerusalem. In His grace and forbearance, God tolerates for a time a certain amount of sin, but then judgment must be passed. This is as true of nations as it is of individuals.

Finally, we read that "a king will arise, insolent and skilled in intrigue." "Insolent" is sometimes translated "fierce of countenance." This man is shameless in carrying out his cruel designs, and he is skilled in intrigue. He is a cunning practitioner of deceit who will succeed for a time in magnifying himself before the Lord God.

Verse 24: When this verse reports that "his power will be mighty," we are reminded that this cannot refer fully to Antiochus, because it was already said that the divided parts of Alexander's empire would never have the power they did when they were united.

This king will be mighty, yet "not by his own power." This lends even more support to the claim that this prophecy did not apply to Antiochus. Rather, this king of the end times will be motivated by satanic power and "will destroy to an extraordinary degree." Even in a world in which destruction has become routine, this king's acts of destruction will be unusual.

Verse 25: This verse stresses how successfully this sinister figure will accomplish his satanic purpose. Largely through his craft and subtlety, he will be more successful in his efforts than Antiochus Epiphanes ever was. We read that "he will magnify himself in his heart"; the fatal flaw in all these rulers during the "times of the Gentiles" is self-promotion. Notice, too, that he secures power for himself by pretending peace and friendship, and then he deals death blows to those who have been lulled into a false sense of security (cf. Jer. 15:8). Once again, this detail of prophecy was not fulfilled by Anitochus, who openly oppressed the Jews; it must await its fulfillment in the future.

This verse goes on to speak of opposing "the Prince of princes." This can mean only God, who rules all the rulers on earth. The result of opposing God is inevitable and is described here as being "broken without human agency." In the original Hebrew, this phrase reads literally, "without hands," and clearly refers to a visitation from God. The power of Antiochus, by contrast, was broken by the heroic exploits of the Maccabees, who were a quite-human agency. In the end times, however, the king of the north will be struck directly by the Lord God, just as will the Antichrist and the beast of Rome. There will be no human intermediary in that day, just the direct infliction of divine wrath.

Verse 26: As Daniel's vision drew to a close, Gabriel assured him that although many days would elapse before it was fulfilled, all these things would in fact come to pass.

I, the LORD, have spoken; it is coming and I shall act. I shall not relent, and I shall not pity, and I shall not be sorry; according to your ways and according to your deeds I shall judge you, declares the Lord GOD [Ezek. 24:14].

Verse 27: Daniel was so amazed at the calamity that was yet to come upon his people that he was physically overcome. It was no ordinary message he had received: the daily sacrifices were to be interrupted, and the worship of the Lord God was to be successfully opposed! This made an enormous impression on Daniel, and it was some time before he had recovered sufficiently to return to the service of the king. The faithful performance of his duties weighed heavily upon him, and we should recognize that being occupied with prophecies of the future did not hinder him from attending to the matters he had at hand.

The man of God who spends time in the prophetic Word will be no less useful to the work of God because of its preoccupation with the things that are to come. Being occupied with heavenly things serves to motivate us to earthly action.

We read in this last verse of the chapter that Daniel was "astounded at the vision," and notice, "there was none to explain it." Apparently, Daniel described something of his vision to others, but they were unable to help him understand it. The general features of the vision were clear enough; but who could supply all the details and declare the precise manner in which all these things would come to pass?

This much is certain. First, no human insight could have foreseen the outline of events set forth in this passage. Second, even those who were eager to know God's plan for the ages could not discern what would occur. And third, when these events did occur, all could admit that this prophecy from God had been correctly foretold. So true is this last fact that Porphyry, an unbeliever who denounced faith in God during the early days of the church, found it necessary to claim that this passage was written after the events they describe; he found it impossible to believe that such detailed predictions could be so accurately fulfilled.

As for believers, we are committed to know these things that describe the role of Israel in the last days. It has been well said that "he who holds closest communion with God is the man best able to carry out the duties of everyday life."

9 The Prophecy of the Seventy Weeks

In the first year of Darius the son of Ahasuerus, of Median descent, who was made king over the kingdom of the Chaldeans—² in the first year of his reign I, Daniel, observed in the books the number of the years which was *revealed as* the word of the LORD to Jeremiah the prophet for the completion of the desolations of Jerusalem, *namely*, seventy years. ³ So I gave my attention to the Lord God to seek *Him* by prayer and supplications, with fasting, sackcloth, and ashes. ⁴ And I prayed to the LORD my God and confessed and said, "Alas, O Lord, the great and awesome God, who keeps His covenant and lovingkindness for those who love Him and keep His commandments, ⁵ we have sinned, committed iniquity, acted wickedly, and rebelled, even turning aside from Thy commandments and ordinances. ⁶ Moreover, we have not listened to Thy servants the prophets, who spoke in Thy name to our kings, our princes, our fathers, and all the people of the land. ⁷ Righteousness belongs to Thee, O Lord, but to us open shame, as it is this day—to the men of Judah, the inhabitants of Jerusalem, and all Israel, those who are near by and those who are far away in all the countries to which Thou hast driven them, because of their unfaithful deeds which they have committed against Thee. ⁸ Open shame belongs to us, O Lord, to our kings, our princes, and our fathers, because we have sinned against Thee. ⁹ To the Lord our God belong compassion and forgiveness, for we have rebelled against Him; ¹⁰ nor have we obeyed the voice of the LORD our God, to walk in His teachings which He set before us through His servants the prophets. ¹¹ Indeed all Israel has transgressed Thy law and turned aside, not obeying Thy voice; so the curse has been poured out on us, along with the oath which is written in the law of Moses the servant of

God, for we have sinned against Him. [12] Thus He has confirmed His words which He had spoken against us and against our rulers who ruled us, to bring on us great calamity; for under the whole heaven there has not been done *anything* like what was done to Jerusalem. [13] As it is written in the law of Moses, all this calamity has come on us; yet we have not sought the favor of the LORD our God by turning from our iniquity and giving attention to Thy truth. [14] Therefore, the LORD has kept the calamity in store and brought it on us; for the LORD our God is righteous with respect to all His deeds which He has done, but we have not obeyed His voice. [15] And now, O Lord our God, who hast brought Thy people out of the land of Egypt with a mighty hand and hast made a name for Thyself, as it is this day—we have sinned, we have been wicked. [16] O Lord, in accordance with all Thy righteous acts, let now Thine anger and Thy wrath turn away from Thy city Jerusalem, Thy holy mountain; for because of our sins and the iniquities of our fathers, Jerusalem and Thy people *have become* a reproach to all those around us. [17] So now, our God, listen to the prayer of Thy servant and to his supplications, and for Thy sake, O Lord, let Thy face shine on Thy desolate sanctuary. [18] O my God, incline Thine ear and hear! Open Thine eyes and see our desolations and the city which is called by Thy name; for we are not presenting our supplications before Thee on account of any merits of our own, but on account of Thy great compassion. [19] O Lord, hear! O Lord, forgive! O Lord, listen and take action! For Thine own sake, O my God, do not delay, because Thy city and Thy people are called by Thy name."

[20] Now while I was speaking and praying, and confessing my sin and the sin of my people Israel, and presenting my supplication before the LORD my God in behalf of the holy mountain of my God, [21] while I was still speaking in prayer, then the man Gabriel, whom I had seen in the vision previously, came to me in *my* extreme weariness about the time of the evening offering. [22] And he gave *me* instruction and talked with me, and said, "O Daniel, I have now come forth to give you insight with understanding. [23] At the beginning of your supplications the command was issued, and I have come to tell *you,* for you are highly esteemed; so give heed to the message and gain understanding of the vision.

[24] "Seventy weeks have been decreed for your people and your holy city, to finish the transgression, to make an end of sin, to make atonement for iniquity, to bring in everlasting righteousness to seal up vision and prophecy, and to anoint the most holy *place*. [25] So you are to know and discern *that* from the issuing of a decree to restore and rebuild Jerusalem until Messiah the Prince *there will be* seven weeks and sixty-two weeks; it will be built again, with plaza and moat, even in times of distress. [26] Then after the sixty-two weeks the Messiah will be cut off and have nothing, and the people of the prince who is to come will destroy the city and the sanctuary. And its end *will come* with a flood; even to the end there will be war; desolations are determined. [27] And he will make a firm covenant with the many for one week, but in the middle of the week he will put a stop to sacrifice and grain offering; and on the wing of abominations *will come* one who makes desolate, even until a complete destruction, one that is decreed, is poured out on the one who makes desolate."

Introduction

We come now to one of the most important chapters of the entire Bible. Sir Edward Denny, a noted nineteenth century student of prophecy, called this passage "the backbone of prophecy." Unless the ninth chapter of the book of Daniel is properly understood, the great prophetic discourse of our Lord Jesus Christ in Matthew 24-25, Mark 13, and Luke 21 will be misunderstood, as will the greater portion of the book of Revelation.

Chapter 9 may be simply divided into three distinct parts: first, Daniel's study of the prophecy of Jeremiah (9:1-2); second, Daniel's prayer for the fulfillment of the prophecy (9:3-19); and third, God's answer to his prayer (9:20-27). **Verse 1:** The events of this chapter occurred "in the first year of Darius the son of Ahasuerus." This was King Cyaxares II, who succeeded Belshazzar and preceded Cyrus the Great. Since Darius reigned before Cyrus, who had issued the order to rebuild the Temple in Jerusalem (Ezra 1:1-3), we know the events of this chapter occurred before the end of the seventy-year-long Babylonian captivity in 536 B.C.

Who is meant by "the son of Ahasuerus"? It was common in the ancient Near East for kings to have more than one name: one writer may have referred to them by one name, and another writer used some other title. In this case, the "son of Ahasuerus" was also known as the "son of Astyages"; we know him today as Darius the Mede.

Verse 2: Daniel had been studying the sacred scrolls (here called books), especially the prophecies of Jeremiah. The prophet's writings had foretold that the Jews would be held captive in Babylon for seventy years (cf. Jer. 25:11-12; 29:10). Thus, although the precise duration of the captivity was known, the precise times of its beginning and end were not. Why was there any question about the exact time of the exile? The confusion arose because King Nebuchadnezzar had invaded Judea three times; any one of those could be interpreted as the beginning of the captivity.

Daniel arrived at the correct conclusion, for just when he expected it, the decree came from Cyrus to rebuild the Temple in Jerusalem. Daniel was rightly concerned about the matter, because he had no way of knowing that Darius would favor returning the Jews to their homeland. Even less could he have known that Cyrus the Persian would soon come to the throne and fulfill Jeremiah's prophecy himself.

These were the conditions that led the godly prophet to turn to God in prayer, asking that He would fulfill His purpose for the Jews. God can turn the heart of a king just as easily as He can turn the rivers in their courses; and the way for us to enter into His blessing is through prayer.

Verse 3: In the original Hebrew, this verse says that Daniel "set his face to the Lord God," which could imply that he directed his prayer toward Jerusalem, as he had done earlier in chapter 6. In fervent prayer, Daniel trusted that God would fulfill His announced purpose.

The matters on Daniel's heart were of vast importance, and the prophet sought to be properly prepared before God by fasting and wearing sackcloth and ashes. Sackcloth was a coarse material used in making sacks and bags, and in those days it was a recognized sign of mourning and humiliation when worn around the loins. In times of sorrow it was also the custom to pour ashes on one's head, probably to conform one's outward appearance to the inward state of one's heart.

This verse teaches that biblical prophecy should bring us to our knees, as it did Daniel. True prayer always seeks to learn God's will in a matter and then prays in conformity with His will.

Verse 4: When Daniel came to God, he not only prayed but also confessed. This is one of the most remarkable statements in the Bible, for Daniel was a man of the purest character. Nevertheless, he humbled himself before God and placed himself in the same position as his apostate people.

Daniel felt responsible for the corporate needs of the Jewish people. Yet before God's blessings are free to descend, the great need in any day is for the people to recognize and confess their sin. If we make any attempt to vindicate ourselves, our actions block His blessing.

Daniel went on to speak of the Lord as "the great and awesome God." This does not mean that God is stern and severe, but rather that He inspires all reverence. Further, the prophet observed that God also "keeps His covenant," that He is faithful and true to His word. If this is not true, there is no value in prayer; in fact, however, if there is any evidence of unfaithfulness in the relationship between man and God, it is on man's part and not God's.

God is not only a covenant-keeping God, but He shows us "lovingkindness" as well. Even when He keeps His covenant, God acts out of grace and mercy toward our sinfulness and faithlessness. However, God is not committed to bless those who practice disobedience. Rather, it is those who obey Him who can expect to find His promises fulfilled. In light of this, then, Daniel could never say that the Jews were obedient and thus had a claim on God; instead, he relied on the mercy of the covenant-keeping God, who remembers His covenant if His people repent.

Verse 5: Daniel confessed to God in the name of the whole nation of Israel, as though he were associating himself with their failure. Certainly, he felt the burden of their sin as keenly as if it had been his own. He described the long series of transgressions that preceded and caused the captivity, and the kinds of expressions he used in his description were meant to convey the intensity of emotion that moved his heart to prayer.

Verse 6: Daniel pointed out here the role that the prophets played in the nation of Israel, namely, to call Israel back to its place of blessing by obedience to the Word of God. The prophets spoke for the Lord and in His name had no respect of persons. But although they faithfully proclaimed the message of divine rebuke both to the king and the common people, Israel would not listen to their warning of coming judgment.

Verse 7: None of the consequences of Israel's sin could be laid to injustice in the Lord. He alone is altogether permeated by righteousness. He alone has been right in every dealing. All the blame and all the shame belonged to Daniel and his people. The rectitude of God's judgments can be depended upon, for He alone does all things righteously.

Verse 8: All had shared the guilt of sin, and all had borne its result.

Verse 9: "To the Lord our God belong compassion and forgiveness." Not only is God righteous in every detail and free from any blame in calamity, but if there are to be any mercies and forgiveness, they can only come from the Lord Himself. The only hope of the people of Israel—and our only hope as well—lay in the mercy and forgiving grace of God, for of itself Israel deserved only unrelieved condemnation. On the basis of our works alone, we have all forfeited the favor and blessings of God (cf. Psalm 25:11; Rom. 3:10-12).

Verse 10: This referred again to the same theme of their disobedience, which was entirely inexcusable in the eyes of God.

Verse 11: Although Israel had been divided for many years, the people were united in their responsibility before the Lord. All had sinned and transgressed against the Lord, and the curse that befell them in consequence was precisely that predicted by Moses in Deuteronomy 28:15-68.

Verse 12: God confirmed His Word by bringing upon the people all that He had threatened if they disobeyed. God ever delights to make good His promises of blessing in reward for obedience; but in His righteousness, He must also fulfill His promises of punishment for disobedience. This is a solemn and sobering thought—or it should be— for all who are unsaved: God is never unmindful of His warnings.

This verse goes on to say, "He ha[s] spoken against us and against our rulers who ruled us." This referred to the magistrates and kings of Israel, who led the nation's apostasy. Daniel then continued in his prayer with the statement, "Under the whole heaven there has not been done anything like what was done to Jerusalem." This was a comprehensive statement that described the slaughter and desolation that was visited upon the people of God.

It is a sure scriptural principle that the greater the amount of light one is given, the greater is one's responsibility to walk by that light and perform the will of God (cf. Luke 12:47-48). In this case, the result for Jerusalem was that the city was destroyed, the Temple left in ruins, and the people either slain or carried into captivity. "A man who hardens his neck after much reproof will suddenly be broken beyond remedy" (Prov. 29:1).

Verse 13: The results of Israel's sin had been according to the exact letter of the Word of God. For despite the fact that Israel failed and sinned, the Israelites did not turn to the Lord in repentance, confess their sin, and petition God for mercy. It was only through such humble petition that they would have discerned the righteous will of God and been restored to His favor (2 Chron. 7:14).

Verse 14: We have here a truth of vital significance to sinners. God keeps His ever watchful eye on the sinner's conduct, and God is righteous in His dealings with it. Daniel's attitude here is an excellent example of the outlook of the godly. In every circumstance and in His every act, God is to be vindicated. This passage clearly shows that Daniel's heart was in proper relation to God, and that the people of Israel suffered only because of their own sin.

Verse 15: Remembrance of God's past blessings on Israel clearly demonstrated how faithful He had been with respect to His covenant with Abraham (see Gen. 15:1-21), and it assures us today that He will continue to grant mercy in the future. Daniel prayed that God had as much reason to intervene on behalf of the Jews in captivity in Babylon as He had had to act on behalf of those in captivity in Egypt; He certainly had lost none of His power to do so. Daniel went on to say that God had "made a name" for Himself through His faithfulness to Israel. His deliverance of the Jews in times past had caused His name to be spread abroad, so that He had become known as the faithful and covenant-keeping God that He is. Further, Daniel observed that God's name and praise had come down through the centuries, "as it is this day," because of such intervention.

The final characterization of Israel's sinfulness and wickedness pointed out strongly the contrast between the Lord's goodness and Israel's ingratitude. Instead of loving Him all the more for His mercies, they had presumptuously sinned against Him all the more. How true this can be of each of us who have tasted so fully of the wonderful grace of our God in the Lord Jesus Christ (cf. Heb. 6:4-6).

Verse 16: Daniel called upon the Lord to act "in accordance with all [His] righteous acts." This referred not to the strict justice of God, but rather to the constant faithfulness the Lord had shown to His unworthy people. Daniel based his pressing plea for help entirely upon the merciful, gracious character of God, and he implored the Lord, "Now Thine anger and Thy wrath turn away." As long as Jerusalem lay in ruins, it symbolized the outpouring wrath of God; but if the Lord were to restore the city and His people, that would symbolize His grace and mercy.

Again, the evidence of this verse is that all of Israel's calamities were the result of its own sin. There is not so much as a hint that Daniel felt as if God had acted unjustly with them. However, since God's name was upon that people, their reproach could have caused the other nations of the world to misinterpret the dealings of God.

Verse 17: Someone has well said that Daniel's argument for the restoration of Israel was based on (1) the confession of sin; (2) the character of God; and (3) the condition of the city and Temple; and it was on behalf of the people. By all these considerations, it pleased God to have mercy on His people and on their land.

When Daniel said, "Let Thy face shine on Thy desolate sanctuary," he asked for the Lord to look with favor and blessing upon His people. The bright sun is a symbol of the grace and favor of God, whereas beclouded skies are a symbol of His wrath.

Daniel prayed that the Lord God would grant his petition for His own sake. This is the highest purpose of prayer, that God might be glorified. His glory outweighs every other conceivable argument or benefit that might appeal to mortal man, and no prayer can ever aspire to anything greater.

Verse 18: Daniel used strongly figurative language as he earnestly pleaded for God to give His attention and favor. After all, the city of Jerusalem did bear the name of the Lord; His glory is inseparably associated with it. Daniel disdained any claims to merit on Israel's part; if God worked, it would have to be solely on the basis of His mercy.

Verse 19: These short, staccato petitions betrayed the intensity and fervor in the prophet's heart. There was certainly no intimation of irreverence or disrespect, but there was the deepest sense of urgency.

Verse 20: If you know God at all through spiritual experience, it is obvious to you that God could not fail to answer Daniel's heartfelt cry. Both in this verse and the next, we read that Daniel's answer came while he was yet praying (cf. Isa. 30:19; 65:24). Before we even ask, God's answer is on the way.

Verse 21: This passage emphasizes the speed with which Daniel's prayer was answered. "The man Gabriel" appeared to Daniel with the Lord's response. Gabriel was here referred to as a man because he took the appearance of one; from Luke 1:19 we know that he is an angel "who stands in the presence of God." He was further designated as the one "whom I had seen in the vision previously." Daniel thus recognized Gabriel from his vision alongside the Ulai Canal (8:1, 16), when he first appeared to the weary prophet.

Gabriel approached Daniel and touched him at "about the time of the evening offering." Although the commanded worship in the Temple was suspended during the entire captivity, Daniel continued to think as if it were still in operation. Ordinarily the Temple was to be used at three o'clock in the afternoon for sacrifice; on this occasion it was employed for prayer.

Verse 22: The angel Gabriel was sent to Daniel to illuminate for him the prophecy of Jeremiah. Beyond that, however, there was also much additional information regarding the last days, which Daniel had not sought.

Verse 23: As soon as the prophet began to pray, God sent Gabriel to reveal to him what was to come in the days ahead; the angel's speed far exceeded that of light. Daniel was "highly esteemed" by God, for he was a man of God's own desire and delight.

This last portion of the chapter demonstrates the remarkable way in which God not only answers prayer, but often answers in a manner that far exceeds expectation. For not only did the Lord answer Daniel's prayer concerning his people, the city of Jerusalem, and the sanctuary; in the last four verses of this chapter, He also unveiled the entire future of God's people, from the end of the Babylonian captivity to the end of time itself.

We cannot overemphasize the importance of this prophecy both for the book of Daniel and for the entire Bible. Unless our understanding is crystal clear here—and it is possible for it to be—we will be unable to understand God's prophetic program in other passages.

In light of this, consider how much God revealed to Daniel in this passage. Through Gabriel, He predicted the restoration of the Jews from the Babylonian captivity to the land of Israel, and the reconstruction of Jerusalem. He prophesied the great opposition that the reconstruction would arouse. He told of the coming of Messiah in the form of a man, His humiliation and violent death. He described the destruction of the Temple in Jerusalem after Messiah's death, the fact that this destruction was to be accomplished by the Romans, and the unstable conditions that were to follow those desolations. Finally, He foretold the disastrous covenant to be made with Rome, the cessation of sacrifices in Israel during the last times, and God's final judgment on those who have desolated His people.

Surely no one could controvert the claim that here is a

prophecy of unusual significance. Let us consider carefully each and every detail.

Verse 24: Daniel had been engrossed with Jeremiah's prophecy of seventy *years* of exile; Gabriel now redirected his attention to another segment of time that he called "seventy *weeks*."

Our initial tendency is to think of a week as a period of seven days, because this is the most common usage for us in the western world. It was not so in Israel. They did have a period of seven days that they called a "week"; but they also had a period of seven years that they also called a "week," or "heptad." An example of this from our own culture would be our use of the word "dozen"; of itself it merely specifies quantity, without indicating what kind of object is being numbered.

How, then, can one decide whether a "week" means seven days or seven years? Not every reference in the Bible to a "week" means seven years; the correct interpretation of each passage must be decided on the basis of its own context, by the trend of that particular portion of Scripture. In this case, the principle of "year-weeks" is found in Numbers 14:34:

> According to the number of days which you spied out the land, forty days, for every day you shall bear your guilt a year, even forty years, and you shall know My opposition.

Other examples of the principle of "year-weeks" may be found in Genesis 29:27, Leviticus 26:34, and Ezekiel 4:6.

These seventy blocks, or heptads, of years add up to 490 years. We read in this verse that these seventy weeks "have been decreed." This term occurs nowhere else in Scripture and means basically "to cut off, to decide, to appoint," and thus, "to determine." The idea here is that this special segment of time had been cut off and set aside for a particular purpose.

As we continue, we read that these seventy weeks had been decreed "for your people and your holy city." These are some of the most important words of the whole prophecy; failure to pay attention to them has led many astray in their interpretations of this passage. Clearly the predictions that follow are solely concerned with Daniel's people—the Jews—and not with the church, which is the Body of Christ. Moreover, they relate also to Daniel's own holy city, which could only mean the holy city of Jerusalem.

During those seventy weeks of years, the great works to be accomplished were: first, "to finish the transgression"; second, "to make an end of sin"; third, "to make atonement for iniquity"; fourth, "to bring in everlasting righteousness"; fifth, "to seal up vision and prophecy"; and sixth, "to anoint the most holy place."

"To finish the transgression" is sometimes interpreted as meaning "to restrain or hold sin back," as though to prevent it from spreading. But it is better to understand it as the removal of sin from God's sight. "To make an end of sin" is to hide it out of sight, and the phrase derives from the custom of sealing up things that were to be concealed. "To make atonement for iniquity" means "to overlay or to cover over sin"; to atone for it, pardon it, forgive it.

Three important Hebrew words for sin were used thus far in this passage. The triple statement concerning sin and Messiah's work in relation to sin deals with the negative aspect of His ministry. In the three other great works that were to be accomplished during the seventy weeks of years, we find the positive aspect of Messiah's ministry.

First, Messiah's work would "bring in everlasting righteousness." He would first provide a basis on which men can become righteous, and then He will set up on earth an eternal kingdom of righteousness. Salvation and righteousness, in fact, are the chief characteristics of Messiah's coming rule on earth (cf. Isa. 45:17; 51:6-8; Jer. 33:14-16).

"To seal up vision and prophecy" refers to giving the seal of confirmation to Daniel and his vision by fulfilling his predictions. In Isaiah 8:16, this phrase meant that the prophecy was complete, and the command was given to bind it up, to roll it up like a scroll and seal it. Again, in Daniel 8:26 the thought was to seal up the prophecy and make a permanent record of it, so that when it is fulfilled the event can be compared to the prophecy to show how completely the one corresponds to the other.

"To anoint the most holy place" has been explained in several ways. It has been suggested at various times that what was meant here was the anointing of the Temple after its defilement by Antiochus Epiphanes; that it referred to the anointing of the temple of the body of Messiah; or that it predicts the anointing of the Temple in Jerusalem after its pollution by the Antichrist. It is better, however, to understand this passage as referring to the millennial temple, which is described in great detail in Ezekiel 40-48.

When we consider the first three great purposes of God for those 490 years, we realize that all three were accomplished by the death of Messiah on the cross for us. But it is imperative that we also recognize that Israel did not partake of these nationally. It would take all 490 years for this to be accomplished for Israel—not just potentially, but actually. Similarly, the last three great purposes of God for those 490 years refer to the fulfillment of this prophecy in the national life of Israel. It cannot be stressed too much that the people and the city spoken of in this passage were those of Daniel. The Gentiles and the church, important entities as they surely are, were not in view here.

Verse 25: Once Gabriel had given Daniel a general overview of the events of the seventy weeks, he elaborated on certain important themes. You may recall that the first statement in verse 24 concerned the time interval of "seventy weeks"; in that passage we were occupied with the events that were to transpire during that time. In this verse, however, the question is, How is that time to be divided, or apportioned? Will there be different segments into which those seventy weeks would be divided? Gabriel exhorted Daniel to "know and discern" the arrangement of the seventy weeks.

The next three verses explain the threefold division of the seventy weeks. The first part would be "seven weeks," or 49 years, long. The second part would be "sixty-two weeks," or 434 years, long. And finally, the third part will be "one week," or seven years, long.

If this timetable is to tell us anything about God's prophetic calendar, we need to know when this period of seventy weeks (or 490 years) began. If our reckoning is incorrect here, no calculations based on this passage will be worth anything.

The beginning of the seventy weeks was definitely given as the time of "the issuing of a decree to restore and rebuild Jerusalem." Which decree was this, and when was it given? It is absolutely essential that we identify the exact decree here referred to.

We know first of all that this decree concerned itself solely with the restoration and reconstruction of Jerusalem. The latter portion of the verse states that "it will be built again, with plaza and moat, even in times of distress." It was in 536 B.C. that Cyrus, upon taking the throne of the Medo-Persian Empire, issued the decree that allowed the Jews to return to Jerusalem. The record of this edict is found in Ezra 1:1-3. It is clear from this passage that his commandment included the reconstruction of the house of the Lord God of Israel and intended nothing more (cf. Ezra 6:15). Thus, that decree cannot be the decree spoken of in Daniel 9:25.

Another imperial decree was the first decree of Artaxerxes, which authorized Ezra to go to Jerusalem on important business. According to Ezra 7:8, this decree was issued

in the seventh year of Artaxerxes' reign. Artaxerxes ruled
the Persian Empire from 465 B.C. to 424 B.C.; thus, the
seventh year of his reign would be 458 B.C. Was that the
decree that Gabriel referred to? We must observe that Ezra
was solely a scribe of the Law of the Lord, instructing the
people of Israel in the Law and statutes of the Lord. Therefore, his calling would not include rebuilding the city of
Jerusalem. Furthermore, we read in Ezra 7:13 that Artaxerxes' decree authorized Ezra only to assemble and conduct to Jerusalem those Jews who were minded to go of
their own free will, and that whatever offerings were entrusted to him were not for rebuilding the city, but were to
be used for the house of the Lord (Ezra 7:15-17). So we see
that every part of this first decree of Artaxerxes was concerned only with matters relating to the Temple; it was not
related in any way to the rebuilding of the city of Jerusalem.

King Artaxerxes Longimanus issued a second decree in
the twentieth year of his reign, 445 B.C. It was given to
Nehemiah, who recorded it in Nehemiah 2:4-8. This,
undoubtedly, was the edict to which Daniel 9:25 refers. In
this second edict there was nothing of the exclusively religious nature of the other two decrees. It dealt solely with a
matter of political import, the rebuilding of the walls of
Jerusalem. We need only read the book of Nehemiah and its
account of his works to know that his activity answered
exactly to the requirements of the decree in Daniel 9:25.

Thus, the seventy weeks of years began in the month of
Nisan (March/April), 445 B.C. We read in verse 25 that the
first division of the seventy weeks was a "seven week," or
49-year-long, period. It is stated that the work to be accomplished during this period was the reconstruction of Jerusalem: "It will be built again, with plaza and moat, even in
times of distress." This perfectly describes the work of
Nehemiah and under what difficult circumstances he performed his tasks.

The second division of the seventy weeks of years was a period of "sixty-two weeks," or 434 years, which had been decreed to be the interval between the edict to rebuild Jerusalem and the coming of "Messiah the Prince." Here we have the exact number of years given in which Messiah, the Hope of Israel, would appear on earth. At that time, "after the sixty-two weeks the Messiah will be cut off and have nothing" (v.26). This was a prediction of the crucifixion of the Lord Jesus Christ on Calvary.

Can we determine whether the predicted 483 years were actually completed when Christ died on the cross? Sir Robert Anderson, a British student of the Word of God, has given us the answer. He notes that the year of Christ's death can be more definitely established than many realize, for the year that our Lord's ministry began is known with certainty. According to Luke 3:1-2, 21, 23, it began "in the fifteenth year of the reign of Tiberius Caesar." Tiberius began his reign on August 19, A.D. 14; thus, the fifteenth year of Tiberius's reign was A.D. 29. The first Passover of our Lord's ministry can therefore be set at Nisan (March/April), A.D. 29, and the date of Messiah's death can be fixed relative to it. The crucifixion took place at the fourth Passover of Jesus' ministry; and, as was the Jewish custom, our Lord went up to Jerusalem on Nisan 8, which fell on a Friday that year. Having passed the Sabbath at Bethany, he entered Jerusalem the next day (cf. John 11:55-12:1; Matt. 21:1-9), which was Sunday, April 6, A.D. 32. Such was the interval between the decree to rebuild Jerusalem and the public advent of Messiah the Prince.

How many days elapsed between March 14, 445 B.C. and April 6, A.D. 32? The calculated interval was exactly 173,880 days, which is equal to 7 times 69 prophetic years of 360 days each (cf. Rev. 12:6, 14). How is this figure arrived at? From 445 B.C. to A.D. 32 is 476 years (since there was no year zero), which is equal to 173,856 days (476 years times 365 days per year, plus 116 days for leap years). Moreover, we must include the interval from March 14 to April 6—reckoned inclusively, according to Jewish practice—which is an additional 24 days. This 24 days, added to the 173,856 days already calculated, totals 173,880 days—the very same number of days as are in 69 weeks of prophetic years. Thus the evidence is complete and undeniable: Messiah was indeed "cut off" after the sixty-two weeks of years were fulfilled.

Verse 26: When we read that Messiah "will have nothing" when He is cut off, it can only mean that He did not receive the Messianic kingdom at that time. When His own people rejected Him (John 1:11), He did not receive what rightly belonged to Him.

Joined with the prediction that Messiah would be cut off was the prophecy of the destruction of the sanctuary and city of Jerusalem. We know this already occurred in A.D. 70, when the Roman army under Titus took the city, inflicted great miseries on the Jews, and reduced it to ashes. From that time until this very day, Jerusalem has not been a completely Jewish city. Even the new part of Jerusalem, held by Jews now, is not part of the old city; and we know as well that part of the old city is today occupied by Arabs.

Years after A.D. 70, Jerusalem was rebuilt as a pagan city. In the fourth century it became nominally Christian, under the Emperor Constantine. Then for a while it became a Persian possession, fell into Muslim hands in A.D. 637, and was captured by the Crusaders in 1099. For more than seven hundred years it was a Muslim city, until after World War I the mandate was given to Great Britain, which then encouraged Jewish occupation of the city.

Our present verse states that both the city and the sanctuary were to be destroyed by "the people of the prince who is to come." Interestingly enough, "the people"—the Romans —have already come, yet "the prince" is still to come. This "prince" cannot refer to "Messiah the Prince" (9:25), since the date of His coming was already so carefully determined. Rather, this refers to a future prince from Rome, who was referred to in chapter 7 as the "little horn" (7:8, 19-26). The final words of verse 26 sum up the history of Israel since A.D. 70: "desolations are determined." Surely the determined wars and desolations have come upon them (cf. Luke 21:24). Such has been the lot of Israel and the city of Jerusalem, and such will be the portion, until the "times of the Gentiles" have been fulfilled.

Verse 27: Thus far we have adequately accounted for 483 of the original 490 years, which are the "seventy weeks" of verse 24. We have seen that those 483 years are now passed, and their predictions have been fulfilled in the crucifixion of Christ and the destruction of Jerusalem.

What about the remaining seven years, the "seventieth week"? Could it have run its course already? That is not possible, since Israel has been out of the land for centuries. Rather, God is not reckoning time for Israel while its people are scattered abroad. For although there is now a state of Israel once again, its population of about three million can scarcely be the full quota of people for the land. No, in this age Israel's prophetic clock has literally stopped, because in this age God is not dealing with the Jews or Gentiles as nations, but strictly on an individual basis. The fact that Israel is in the land once again shows that God may very soon begin dealing with them on a national basis; when He does, the church will be home in glory.

So, after the first 483 years had passed, an indefinite, unforeseen period of time has followed. When that interval has expired—and absolutely no one knows when that will be—the last seven years of this prophecy will run their declared course.

Who is it that makes "a firm covenant with the many" for this last, seven year period? There are some who believe that the one who makes the covenant is the Lord Jesus Christ. Nothing could be further from the truth, however. Christ did make a covenant, but it was never to last for only seven years: it is an eternal covenant, made for the benefit of His own (Luke 22:20). Both logically and grammatically, the "he" of verse 27 must refer to "the prince who is to come" of verse 26.

The head of the revived Roman empire will be the one to "make a firm covenant with the many" in Israel. There will be godly Israelites who will refuse to enter into this agreement with the Roman prince, and they will suffer for their faithful stand. After the first half of the seventieth week, the Roman beast will break his promise; how easily this is done we know only too well by observing the international scene today. And how will he break his covenant with the many in Israel? He will cause the whole ceremonial system in Jerusalem to cease.

This ruler will be motivated by the power of Satan; in collaboration with the religious leader, the Antichrist in Jerusalem, he will introduce shocking idolatry in place of the regular sacrifice and worship of the Temple. At that point, the terrors of the last three and one-half years will be upon Israel. Daniel 7:25 refers to this length of time as "a time, times, and half a time." In the book of Revelation, it is spoken of as "forty-two months" (Rev. 11:2; 13:5) and as "twelve hundred and sixty days" (Rev. 11:3; 12:6). The activities of the Roman ruler during this period are described in Revelation 13:1-10, and those of the Antichrist follow immediately in Revelation 13:11-17. Their idolatry will have the power of Satan behind it, fostering it.

The "abominations" refers to this idolatry that will be introduced in the last days, when the Roman ruler will make his will known under its protection. At that point, the prophecy spoken by our Lord in Matthew 12:43-45 will be fulfilled, and because of this defiant idolatry, desolation will befall the land. God in His wrath will ultimately deal with the desolator. The great prophetic discourse of our Lord, recorded in Matthew 24-25, Mark 13, and Luke 21, tells us of the course of events during this period of Israel's history. How far away are these things that have been predicted? We repeat that no one knows, but it is imperative to be ready through faith in the Lord Jesus Christ. Each year we live—yes, each day!—the time draws closer to these events. Time is running out for this age; we have been granted to live to see remarkable signs of the revival of Israel's national history. Never doubt it: all that God has foretold will come to pass, and in the same literal manner He has indicated. Is not this chapter one of the most remarkable in the entire Bible? And just as some of it has already been fulfilled, so you may be sure that the Lord will also bring the rest to pass.

When we survey the great scope of this prophecy and the wealth of detail it contains, we can only conclude that it is the product of divine inspiration. To predict events thousands of years in the future with such exactitude is a feat far beyond the insight and sagacity of the natural man; it is the product of the mind and heart of Him who knows all things from the beginning.

10 The Delayed Answer to Prayer

In the third year of Cyrus king of Persia a message was revealed to Daniel, who was named Belteshazzar; and the message was true and *one of* great conflict, but he understood the message and had an understanding of the vision. ² In those days I, Daniel, had been mourning for three entire weeks. ³ I did not eat any tasty food, nor did meat or wine enter my mouth, nor did I use any ointment at all, until the entire three weeks were completed. ⁴ And on the twenty-fourth day of the first month, while I was by the bank of the great river, that is, the Tigris, ⁵ I lifted my eyes and looked, and behold, there was a certain man dressed in linen, whose waist was girded with *a belt of* pure gold of Uphaz. ⁶ His body also was like beryl, his face had the appearance of lightning, his eyes were like flaming torches, his arms and feet like the gleam of polished bronze, and the sound of his words like the sound of a tumult. ⁷ Now I, Daniel, alone saw the vision, while the men who were with me did not see the vision; nevertheless, a great dread fell on them, and they ran away to hide themselves. ⁸ So I was left alone and saw this great vision; yet no strength was left in me, for my natural color turned to a deathly pallor, and I retained no strength. ⁹ But I heard the sound of his words; and as soon as I heard the sound of his words, I fell into a deep sleep on my face, with my face to the ground.

¹⁰ Then behold, a hand touched me and set me trembling on my hands and knees. ¹¹ And he said to me, "O Daniel, man of high esteem, understand the words that I am about to tell you and stand upright, for I have now been sent to you." And when he had spoken this word to me, I stood up trembling. ¹² Then he said to me, "Do not be afraid, Daniel, for from the first day that you set your heart on understanding *this* and on humbling yourself be-

137

fore your God, your words were heard, and I have come in response to your words. ¹³ But the prince of the kingdom of Persia was withstanding me for twenty-one days; then behold, Michael, one of the chief princes, came to help me, for I had been left there with the kings of Persia. ¹⁴ Now I have come to give you an understanding of what will happen to your people in the latter days, for the vision pertains to the days yet *future*." ¹⁵ And when he had spoken to me according to these words, I turned my face toward the ground and became speechless. ¹⁶ And behold, one who resembled a human being was touching my lips; then I opened my mouth and spoke, and said to him who was standing before me, "O my lord, as a result of the vision anguish has come upon me, and I have retained no strength. ¹⁷ "For how can such a servant of my lord talk with such as my lord? As for me, there remains just now no strength in me, nor has any breath been left in me."

¹⁸ Then *this* one with human appearance touched me again and strengthened me. ¹⁹ And he said, "O man of high esteem, do not be afraid. Peace be with you; take courage and be courageous!" Now as soon as he spoke to me, I received strength and said, "May my lord speak, for you have strengthened me." ²⁰ Then he said, "Do you understand why I came to you? But I shall now return to fight against the prince of Persia; so I am going forth, and behold, the prince of Greece is about to come. ²¹ However, I will tell you what is inscribed in the writing of truth. (Yet there is no one who stands firmly with me against these *forces* except Michael your prince.)"

Introduction

The tenth chapter of the book of Daniel forms an introduction to the messages of chapters 11 and 12. In these last three chapters of the book, we will again find a wealth of prophetic detail that describes world history until its conclusion in the kingdom of Messiah.

Verse 1: In Daniel 1:21, we were told, "Daniel continued until the first year of Cyrus the king," but that does not

necessarily mean Daniel died then. An alternative interpretation could be that Daniel continued until that time in
his official capacity; certainly he could have lived for several
years beyond that. Indeed, in this passage we are taken two
years beyond the statement of Daniel 1:21 to "the third year
of Cyrus king of Persia." But regardless of whether he held
positions of prominence, Daniel never allowed his love and
concern for the nation of Israel to wane.

We read in this first verse that the message from God was
revealed to "Daniel, who was named Belteshazzar." This
serves to identify the author, despite the fact that the
Babylonian Empire had been replaced by the Persian Empire; his own countrymen would have recognized him by
that name. Next, we read that this message from God "was
true"; it would certainly be fulfilled, regardless of whether
the prophet himself were to pass from the earthly scene.

This verse goes on to say that the message from God was
"one of great conflict." This concept is the keynote of the
revelations that were revealed to the prophet in these last
three chapters. They center on great warfare and the evils
and hardships of war.

Finally, we are told that Daniel "understood the message
and had an understanding of the vision." This is evidently
stated in contrast to the other occasions, when Daniel did
not understand the meaning of what was revealed to him. In
this case, however, he fully comprehended what the Spirit
of God was disclosing to him. This narrative is very detailed
and is of a historical character, which may account for the
fact that there was little doubt about its meaning. It took
place two years after the Jewish exiles left Babylon, at the
time when they had begun to experience the "times of
distress" spoken of in Daniel 9:25.

Verses 2 and 3: We are not told what the prophet's concern
was, but it was doubtless the condition of his people. When
we read that he fasted "for three entire weeks," these are

literally three weeks of days: abstaining from food, wine, and oil were outward signs of grief. Fasting is not an indispensable Christian obligation, but it is an outward expression of sorrow for sin and of separation from ordinary worldly pleasures in order to give oneself more fully to prayer (cf. Acts 13:2-3).

Verse 4: It was at the end of three weeks of fasting and praying that Daniel received the vision that follows. This occurred in the month of Nisan, which was an appropriate time to consider Israel's calamity, for in it came the Feast of the Passover that commemorated Israel's liberation from bondage. We are told that this vision occurred "by the bank of the great river, that is, the Tigris." The Akkadian name for this river was the Hiddekel. It was unusual for the Tigris to be called "the great river"; generally, that title was applied to the Euphrates. In studying this passage, there is no reason to believe that Daniel was there in a trance, but was rather there in full, waking reality.

Verse 5: While he was engaged in deep thought and meditation, Daniel lifted up his eyes and saw an angel, again in the form of a man (cf. Dan. 8:15). Linen was the most common apparel of priests and is also known as the raiment of angels (Rev. 15:6). In the east it was customary, then as now, to wear a girdle around one's loins, and the one described here was of the finest gold. The name "Uphaz" is mentioned only here and in Jeremiah 10:9, so nothing is known of its identity.

Verse 6: The description of the angel who appeared to Daniel is important, because it goes into considerable detail. The beryl is a very hard mineral and is said to be identical with the emerald, except that the emerald has a purer and richer color. The angel's face was bright, his eyes penetrating; his arms and feet were as bright as burnished metal, his voice loud and powerful. This description is too majestic and exalted to be that of an ordinary angel, and it bears an extraordinary resemblance to that of our Savior as He appeared to John on Patmos (Rev. 1). It undoubtedly describes the Angel of the Lord, the Angel of the covenant, the Lord Jesus Christ.

Verse 7: We read here, "I, Daniel, alone saw the vision." Only the prophet was privileged to receive the vision, while others heard only that which terrified them and caused them to flee. This passage reminds us somewhat of the apostle Paul's experience on the road to Damascus (cf. Acts 9:3-9).

Verse 8: Again, Daniel emphasized that he alone saw the vision. Although he had received revelations from God before, he was completely overcome by what he saw (cf. Rev. 1:17). There was no strength left in him, and he paled with a deathly pallor.

Verse 9: What the prophet heard was so overpowering that he sank senseless to the ground.

Verse 10: With the Angel's help, Daniel was able to recover somewhat, but notice that he was not yet able to stand erect; his strength was restored to him only gradually.

Verse 11: The Angel's encouragement helped him finally to stand upright, yet Daniel was still not fully recovered from his fright.

Verse 12: Daniel was again reassured so that he need not fear the presence of the Angel or fear that his prayers went unheard. On the contrary, Daniel's prayers were heard from the first day he offered them; but he could not receive the answer to them sooner, for reasons given in the next verse.

This verse constitutes a great encouragement to those whose prayers are not answered immediately. The cause of the delay may be something totally unknown to us; yet although the answer may be delayed, the prayer is always heard immediately.

In Daniel's case, the messenger bringing the answer to prayer was delayed. Daniel certainly would have been cheered while he was fasting had he only known that the Angel was on His way to comfort him and bring him the revelation from God. But it is often in the times of our greatest anxiety—when we do not seem to be getting through to heaven, when we have no answer at all, when everything seems to be kept from us—that we must realize that God is still working to answer our prayers, and that a messenger of His could well be on the way to gladden our hearts and wipe away our tears.

Verse 13: It has been said that there is no single verse in the whole of Scripture that speaks more clearly than this about the invisible powers that rule and influence nations.

We read here that the Angel was delayed because "the prince of the kingdom of Persia" opposed him for twenty-one days. In the original language, the phrase "the prince of the kingdom of Persia" might refer to a prince or prime minister who ruled over the kingdom of Persia; but the language and context of this passage are such that it could also apply to a spiritual being who presides over a state and influences its policy. Since such an angelic being was speaking, it is most natural to infer that He was met by another angelic being. The mention of the archangel Michael strengthens this position.

The Angel was delayed because this other spiritual being "was withstanding me for twenty-one days." He was resisted and opposed in His mission and was thus delayed on His way to convey the message to Daniel. We are not told in what manner this resistance was exercised; however, it seems that in order to answer Daniel's prayers for his people, it was necessary for some influence to be brought to bear on the Persian government. Only then could the Jews be restored to their native land.

It is no coincidence that Daniel spent "twenty-one days" praying and fasting, for it took all that time for the Angel to overcome the spiritual resistance to God's plan for His people. The archangel Michael, who helped overcome that resistance, is the first in rank among all the angels; but he is in no sense divine. He is revealed in Scripture as the patron and champion of Daniel's people (see Dan. 12:1) and is referred to here as "one of the chief princes." The manner in which Michael helped the Angel is not specified, but it is implied by the broader context of this book that he helped obtain from the Persian government more-favorable policies relative to the Jews. It took supernatural power to influence the leaders of the Persian Empire so that they might be favorably disposed toward the Jews and permit their restoration to the land of Israel.

Reading further, we find that the Angel "had been left there with the kings of Persia." The exact meaning of this is that the Angel prevailed, or gained the ascendancy, over the opposing angel of Persia. Thus, with Michael's help the Angel secured favor for the people of Israel, for which Daniel had so long and earnestly prayed.

This passage should teach us that there are numerous hindrances of which we are totally unaware to the answering of our prayers. It is our duty, therefore, to be patient, realizing that God always hears our prayers, even when the answer is long delayed.

Verse 14: When the Angel finally did arrive, He announced His purpose as being "to give you an understanding of what will happen to your people in the latter days." This phrase "in the latter days" reminds us again that although this prophecy related to events of Daniel's day, its final significance attaches to the end of Israel's history in the establishment of the Messianic kingdom on earth. Further evidence of this is found in the statement, "The vision pertains to the days yet future." Although Daniel's petitions may have concerned themselves only with Israel's immediate future, the Angel's disclosure included a much more extended period of time. Answers to prayer are often such; they frequently include much more than was originally asked for.

Verse 15: The prophet was again overcome by the truth

that was revealed to him. Perhaps Daniel's actions were no longer to be ascribed to fear, for that had been removed from him (v. 12). Instead, we may understand his actions as reverence for the Person who was majestically standing before him, and as gratitude for the answer to his prayer.

Verse 16: We read here, "Behold, one who resembled a human being was touching my lips." This was an angel in the form of a man. Some have said that it was Gabriel who appeared to Daniel again in the form of a man (cf. Dan. 8:16-17), but there is no reason why it may not be the same One who was speaking to Daniel already. Why he was not identified more specifically is not known.

The prophet, having been delivered from his fear, addressed his statement to the angelic visitor. By calling the Angel "my lord," Daniel was not ascribing to him deity but was merely using the words as an expression of respect. When he said, "As a result of the vision anguish has come upon me," Daniel used the same expression that is used of a woman travailing in childbirth.

Verse 17: Daniel acknowledged his own lowly and humble condition in the presence of the Angel. "As for me," he said, "there remains just now no strength in me, nor has any breath been left in me." He considered himself incapable of speaking in the presence of One who had come from God.

Verse 18: Because the prophet was only gradually recovering his strength, it was necessary for the Angel to come and strengthen him further. He was now prepared to receive the divine communication with a quiet spirit.

Verse 19: The Angel said to Daniel, "Do not be afraid." There was no reason for Daniel to be afraid—either of the Angel Himself or of the message He was soon to give. Daniel went on to report that "as soon as he spoke to me, I received strength." He had been told to "take courage and be courageous," words normally used for those who are timid or weak. By now, however, Daniel had been sufficiently strengthened to receive the message.

Verse 20: The Angel's question was pointed in view of what He said in verse 14. He did, in fact, call Daniel's attention to the general significance of the disclosures that were to follow. So He said, "I shall now return to fight against the prince of Persia." After He had delivered to Daniel the predictions concerning the latter days, He prepared to return to fight the prince of Persia.

Apparently, the struggle with the prince of Persia was not entirely settled, so the Angel needed to set the matter right, permanently. There were yet factors in Persia that could frustrate God's plan for Israel if they were allowed to continue unchecked. The Angel had to return, therefore, to counteract those factors and assure the safe return of the Jews to their homeland.

When the Angel did go forth, world affairs would follow a very different course. The "prince of Greece" would appear, and through him the cause of the Jews would be favored. The meaning of this passage was that until the "prince of Greece" appeared, events would require the direct intervention of heaven in the affairs of Israel. But when the "prince of Greece" came, he would be kindly disposed toward the Jews and their political condition. There is no question but that the "prince of Greece" referred to here was Alexander the Great (cf. Dan. 8:21). It is a matter of historical record that Alexander favored the Jews. With his advent, whatever the people of God had to fear was removed.

Verse 21: In this last verse of the chapter, the Angel told Daniel, "I will tell you what is inscribed in the writing of truth." This doubtless referred to the divine decrees of all future events, which are inscribed in a book in God's own keeping. The Angel came to disclose to Daniel some of the truth in that volume, to disclose a series of events that were and are of vital interest to Israel and the world.

The Angel declared to Daniel, "There is no one who stands firmly with me...except Michael your prince." There were great forces arrayed against God's purpose for Israel; yet no one was disposed to help Him except the archangel Michael, the patron and guardian of Israel. Michael has special concern for the people of Israel and is their protector in time of trouble. That is an important truth that is too little recognized by the world and whose full force is seldom appreciated even by believers.

Summary

This tenth chapter makes a significant contribution to our understanding of how unseen spiritual forces relate to earthly affairs. The veil is drawn aside as we learn of the powers that oppose the people of God. Earthly events are of interest to angelic beings, for earth is the battleground of the war between the forces of good and evil.

As Daniel was exhorted to be patient, so should we also persevere in the Lord as He tests our faith. This chapter is a wonderful encouragement to persevere in prayer. Real prayer is heard by God at once, although the answer may at times be delayed in reaching us. Prayer delayed, as has been said many times, is not prayer denied. Pray on with confidence in the promises of our blessed God. And finally, how blessed we are to know that the rulers and governments of men are all under the wise and able guidance of God. He restrains where necessary, encourages where necessary, and works all things to the glory of His name and for the good of His own.

11 The Wars of the Ptolemies and the Seleucidae, and Antichrist

"(And in the first year of Darius the Mede, I arose to be an encouragement and a protection for him.) ² And now I will tell you the truth. Behold, three more kings are going to arise in Persia. Then a fourth will gain far more riches than all *of them;* as soon as he becomes strong through his riches, he will arouse the whole *empire* against the realm of Greece. ³ And a mighty king will arise, and he will rule with great authority and do as he pleases. ⁴ But as soon as he has arisen, his kingdom will be broken up and parceled out toward the four points of the compass, though not to his *own* descendants, nor according to his authority which he wielded; for his sovereignty will be uprooted and *given* to others besides them. ⁵ Then the king of the South will grow strong, along with *one* of his princes who will gain ascendancy over him and obtain dominion; his domain *will be* a great dominion *indeed.* ⁶ And after some years they will form an alliance, and the daughter of the king of the South will come to the king of the North to carry out a peaceful arrangement. But she will not retain her position of power, nor will he remain with his power, but she will be given up, along with those who brought her in, and the one who sired her, as well as he who supported her in *those* times. ⁷ But one of the descendants of her line will arise in his place, and he will come against *their* army and enter the fortress of the king of the North, and he will deal with them and display *great* strength. ⁸ And also their gods with their metal images *and* their precious vessels of silver and gold he will take into captivity to Egypt, and he on his part will refrain from *attacking* the king of the North for *some* years. ⁹ Then the latter will enter the realm of the king of the South, but will return to his *own* land.

¹⁰ "And his sons will mobilize and assemble a multitude of great

forces; and one of them will keep on coming and overflow and pass through, that he may again wage war up to his *very* fortress. ¹¹ And the king of the South will be enraged and go forth and fight with the king of the North. Then the latter will raise a great multitude, but *that* multitude will be given into the hand of the *former.* ¹² When the multitude is carried away, his heart will be lifted up, and he will cause tens of thousands to fall; yet he will not prevail. ¹³ For the king of the North will again raise a greater multitude than the former, and after an interval of some years he will press on with a great army and much equipment.

¹⁴ "Now in those times many will rise up against the king of the South; the violent ones among your people will also lift themselves up in order to fulfill the vision, but they will fall down. ¹⁵ Then the king of the North will come, cast up a siege mound, and capture a well-fortified city; and the forces of the South will not stand *their ground,* not even their choicest troops, for there will be no strength to make a stand. ¹⁶ But he who comes against him will do as he pleases, and no one will *be able to* withstand him; he will also stay *for a time* in the Beautiful Land, with destruction in his hand. ¹⁷ And he will set his face to come with the power of his whole kingdom, bringing with him a proposal of peace which he will put into effect; he will also give him the daughter of women to ruin it. But she will not take a stand *for him* or be on his side. ¹⁸ Then he will turn his face to the coastlands and capture many. But a commander will put a stop to his scorn against him; moreover, he will repay him for his scorn. ¹⁹ So he will turn his face toward the fortresses of his own land, but he will stumble and fall and be found no more.

²⁰ "Then in his place one will arise who will send an oppressor through the Jewel of *his* kingdom; yet within a few days he will be shattered, though neither in anger nor in battle. ²¹ And in his place a despicable person will arise, on whom the honor of kingship has not been conferred, but he will come in a time of tranquility and seize the kingdom by intrigue. ²² And the overflowing forces will be flooded away before him and shattered, and also the prince of the covenant. ²³ And after an alliance is made with him he will practice deception, and he will go up and gain power with a small *force of* people. ²⁴ In a time of tranquility he will enter the richest

parts of the realm, and he will accomplish what his fathers never did, nor his ancestors; he will distribute plunder, booty, and possessions among them, and he will devise his schemes against strongholds, but *only* for a time. [25] And he will stir up his strength and courage against the king of the South with a large army; so the king of the South will mobilize an extremely large and mighty army for war; but he will not stand, for schemes will be devised against him. [26] And those who eat his choice food will destroy him, and his army will overflow, but many will fall down slain. [27] As for both kings, their hearts will be *intent* on evil, and they will speak lies *to each other* at the same table; but it will not succeed, for the end is still *to come* at the appointed time. [28] Then he will return to his land with much plunder; but his heart will be *set* against the holy covenant, and he will take action and *then* return to his *own* land.

[29] "At the appointed time he will return and come into the South, but this last time it will not turn out the way it did before. [30] For ships of Kittim will come against him; therefore he will be disheartened, and will return and become enraged at the holy covenant and take action; so he will come back and show regard for those who forsake the holy covenant. [31] And forces from him will arise, desecrate the sanctuary fortress, and do away with the regular sacrifice. And they will set up the abomination of desolation. [32] And by smooth *words* he will turn to godlessness those who act wickedly toward the covenant, but the people who know their God will display strength and take action. [33] And those who have insight among the people will give understanding to the many; yet they will fall by sword and by flame, by captivity and by plunder, for *many* days. [34] Now when they fall they will be granted a little help, and many will join with them in hypocrisy. [35] And some of those who have insight will fall, in order to refine, purge, and make them pure, until the end time; because *it is* still *to come* at the appointed time.

[36] "Then the king will do as he pleases, and he will exalt and magnify himself above every god, and will speak monstrous things against the God of gods; and he will prosper until the indignation is finished, for that which is decreed will be done. [37] And he will show no regard for the gods of his fathers or for the desire of

women, nor will he show regard for any *other* god; for he will magnify himself above *them* all. [38] But instead he will honor a god of fortresses, a god whom his fathers did not know; he will honor *him* with gold, silver, costly stones, and treasures. [39] And he will take action against the strongest of fortresses with *the help of* a foreign god; he will give great honor to those who acknowledge *him,* and he will cause them to rule over the many, and will parcel out land for a price.

[40] "And at the end time the king of the South will collide with him, and the king of the North will storm against him with chariots, with horsemen, and with many ships; and he will enter countries, overflow *them,* and pass through. [41] He will also enter the Beautiful Land, and many *countries* will fall; but these will be rescued out of his hand: Edom, Moab and the foremost of the sons of Ammon. [42] Then he will stretch out his hand against *other* countries, and the land of Egypt will not escape. [43] But he will gain control over the hidden treasures of gold and silver, and over all the precious things of Egypt; and Libyans and Ethiopians *will follow* at his heels. [44] But rumors from the East and from the North will disturb him, and he will go forth with great wrath to destroy and annihilate many. [45] And he will pitch the tents of his royal pavilion between the seas and the beautiful Holy Mountain; yet he will come to his end, and no one will help him."

Introduction

The material in this eleventh chapter of the book of Daniel is a part of the things that the Angel said were "inscribed in the writing of truth" (Dan. 10:21). The disclosures made here cover a large portion of the ancient history of Israel, as well as an important period in the future history of the world. The events described in this chapter lead ultimately to the end of world history as we know it, to the end of all things.

First, this chapter sketches the succession of the kings of Persia and their conflicts with the power of Greece. Second, the kingdom of Greece produces a ruler of global stature, who is described. Third, this passage describes the decline of this Greek leader's empire following his death. Fourth, this history outlines the conflict between two parts of the former Greek empire, namely, the "king of the North" (Syria) and the "king of the South" (Egypt). Finally, the chapter describes at length the character and deeds of one of those kings, the "king of the North," Antiochus Epiphanes. We studied Antiochus Epiphanes in the eighth chapter of this book and saw that he prefigures the main religious leader of the end times, the Antichrist.

A great wealth of detail is revealed to us in this chapter of Scripture; it is truly a marvel of divine inspiration. The events prophesied in this chapter are traced as accurately as one would have expected from a history of those times written *after* the fact.

Verse 1: The Angel continued His revelation to Daniel with the account that, "in the first year of Darius the Mede, I arose to be an encouragement and a protection for him." We are not told how the Angel strengthened Darius, but it was undoubtedly related to the restoration of the Jews to their homeland and the rebuilding of their Temple.

The events described in chapter 9 are relevant here. As was seen in that passage, the influence that God exercised on the heart of King Darius led him to issue the edict that permitted the Jews to return to Israel and rebuild the Temple. Cyrus the Persian actually issued the decree, but his uncle Darius was the source of its authority (cf. Dan. 6:8-9, commentary).

Notice that the Angel's purpose was "to be an encouragement and a protection for him." The king had not fully arrived at a decision regarding the Jews, for there were powerful spiritual forces at work in Persia to defeat the purposes of God. As we saw in the last chapter, however, the Angel went to battle there; and we learn further in this passage that He helped to confirm and stabilize Darius in the purpose the Lord had decreed.

Verse 2: The Angel proceeded to tell Daniel the truth of things yet to transpire. First, "three more kings are going to arise in Persia." After Cyrus the Persian died in 529 B.C., he was succeeded by Cambyses, Bardiya (also known as the Pseudo-Smerdis), and Darius Hystaspes. When this verse says that after the first three kings, "a fourth will gain far more riches than all of them," that undoubtedly referred to Xerxes. Although there were other Persian kings after Xerxes, it was he who stirred up the wrath of Greece by his invasion. He prepared his expedition into Greece for four years, gathering and equipping what was probably one of the largest armies ever assembled. According to one source, Xerxes' army numbered some one million men.

When this verse states that he "will gain far more riches" than all those who had preceded him, it offers an accurate description of Xerxes. He inherited the wealth accumulated by previous kings, since he was the son and successor of Darius; and their campaigns of conquest were some of the most remunerative in history.

Verse 3: After this, "a mighty king will arise." Notice that this text does not state that this king would arise from Persia, as the other three had. From the next verse it is clear that this referred instead to the king of Macedon, Alexander the Great.

In a letter to Darius the Mede, Alexander wrote:

Your ancestors entered into Macedonia and the other parts of Greece, and did us damage when they had received no affront to cause it. Now I, as General of the Greeks, and provoked by you and desirous of avenging the injury done us by the Persians, have passed into Asia.

Alexander conquered many great armies and vast territories and felt that on that basis all were to be subordinate to him. His actions and rulings were quite arbitrary, and thus in this verse it was prophesied that "he will rule with great authority and do as he pleases."

The ancient historian Flavius Josephus recorded that the Jewish high priest showed this passage of prophetic Scripture to Alexander himself, and that this was responsible for the conqueror's favorable attitude toward the Jews. However, no other record of this has been found.

Verse 4: At the height of its power, when its influence was universally felt, the Hellenistic Empire of Alexander the Great was shattered by the unexpected, untimely death of its founder at the age of thirty-three. His empire did not gradually decay and decline, but rather it was divided into four parts, "toward the four points of the compass."

One would normally expect Alexander's throne to be passed on to his descendants; but his two lawful sons and heirs, Hercules and Alexander, were murdered and thus kept from the throne. That fulfilled the prophecy contained in this verse that Alexander's power would be parceled out, "though not to his own descendants,...for his sovereignty will be uprooted and given to others besides them." Finally, we read that Alexander's empire would not be continued "according to his authority which he wielded." None of Alexander's successors ever exercised the power of command that he had, and the four parts of his former empire gradually weakened and decayed.

Verse 5: The Angel left the overall history of the Hellenistic Empire and restricted Himself to two of its four parts: the kingdom of the north and the kingdom of the south.

In Scripture, directional references are always relative to Palestine. Thus, the "kingdom of the North" is to be identified with the Seleucid Dynasty of Syria, and the "kingdom of the South" with the Ptolemaic Dynasty of Egypt. The futures of these two lands are important, since they border on the Land of Promise.

In this chapter, the numerous references to the king of the north and the king of the south do not all refer to the same two kings, but to several different kings in each of the two dynasties. Many different battles were fought between

these two Hellenistic kingdoms over a period of several
centuries, and during that time a number of different kings
fulfilled the prophecies in this passage.

In this verse, the "king of the South" referred to King
Ptolemy Lagus, whose strength and dominion are well-
attested by history. We read that he "will grow strong, along
with one of his princes." This prince may have been Ptolemy, who was one of Alexander's princes, or, as is more
likely, it may have been Seleucus I, called Nicator. Seleucus
Nicator was subject to Ptolemy at first, for Ptolemy con-
trolled the greatest of the four parts into which Alexander's
empire had been partitioned. When Ptolemy died, however, conditions changed under his successor, Ptolemy Soter.
Seleucus was able to annex Babylonia, Media, and surround-
ing territories and was then in a position to throw off his
allegiance to Egypt and rule independently.

Verse 6: Naturally, this caused warfare to erupt between the
Ptolemies and the Seleucidae, yet our text goes on to say
that "after some years they will form an alliance." After some
initial hostilities, both kingdoms would attempt to settle
their differences by intermarriage of the royal families. This
prophecy was fulfilled when Berenice, the daughter of
Ptolemy Philadelphus, married Antiochus Theos, who was
then the Seleucid king.

Ptolemy had given his daughter in marriage to Antiochus
Theos in the hope of bringing peace to the two embattled
kingdoms, but it was not to be. One of the conditions of the
treaty had been that Antiochus would divorce his wife
Laodice, and that the children by that marriage would be
blocked from succession to his throne. Only the children of
Antiochus's marriage to Berenice were to be in the royal
line, thus uniting the two kingdoms of Syria and Egypt.

The plan failed, however, for Ptolemy died two years after
Berenice's marriage. In his absence, Antiochus put Berenice
away and restored Laodice as his queen. Laodice feared the

fickleness of her husband's affections, however, and murdered him to protect herself. The officers of Antiochus's court then plotted the deaths of Berenice and her children, who fled to Daphne in a vain effort to save their lives. It was there, however, that they were all put to death by poison. Thus, instead of the succession to the Seleucid throne going to Berenice's children, they were all put to death. As this verse had prophesied, "She will not retain her position of power." We read further, "Nor will he remain with his power." The plans of King Ptolemy of Egypt to bring Syria under his control would never materialize.

Finally, we read that "she will be given up, along with those who brought her in, and the one who sired her, as well as he who supported her in those times." This last part of the prophecy was fulfilled when Berenice was given over to death at Laodice's command. Her entire retinue of attendants, her children, and her father, Ptolemy, were all "given up," just as the Scripture had predicted.

Verse 7: "But one of the descendants of her line will arise in his place, and he will come against their army." The expression "one of the descendants of her line" reminds one of Isaiah 11:1 and refers to one of common stock, or the same family, as Berenice. This relative of Berenice's was to "come against" the king of the north with his army, and he would prevail against him.

This prophecy was fulfilled when Berenice's death was avenged by her brother, Ptolemy Euergetes of Egypt. As soon as he heard what was happening to his sister in Syria, he mustered his army out of Egypt. He originally intended to rescue Berenice, but by the time he arrived with his army, it was too late to save her. Ptolemy Euergetes then undertook to avenge her death in a campaign of conquest, and he succeeded in subduing Syria, Cilicia, and Mesopotamia as far as the river Tigris. When he returned to Egypt in triumph, he brought with him the great wealth that he had plundered abroad. After Laodice brought about the death of Antiochus Theos, she had her son, Seleucus II Callinicus, crowned in his place.

Verse 8: As we have seen, Ptolemy Euergetes took from his conquests great spoils of every kind. Jerome claims that when he returned to Egypt, Ptolemy brought with him 40,000 talents of silver and 2,400 gold vessels and images. Among these were many Egyptian idols that Cambyses had taken to Persia when he conquered Egypt in 525 B.C. By returning these sacred artifacts to their rightful places, Ptolemy endeared himself to the people of Egypt. It was for this reason that he was given the additional name of Euergetes, which means "benefactor."

We read further, "He on his part will refrain from attacking the king of the North for some years." It is probably better to read the text here, "He shall continue more years than the king of the North." Actually, Ptolemy Euergetes survived Seleucus II Callinicus by about four years, having ruled Egypt for twenty-five years.

Verse 9: This simply states that after all his exploits and endeavors, the king of the south would return to his own land of Egypt and remain there with the fruits of his labors.

Verse 10: We read here, "His sons will mobilize and assemble a multitude of great forces." This referred to the sons of Seleucus II Callinicus, who died when he fell from his horse. His sons were known as Callinicus II Ceraunus and Antiochus III the Great. Callinicus Ceraunus died soon after his father, leaving the throne to his fifteen-year-old brother.

Antiochus carried on the war with Egypt, as this verse predicted. In the critical conflict with Egypt, the Seleucidae summoned every force at their command. Once assembled, that force would "keep on coming and overflow and pass through." The change in this verse from the plural "his sons" to the singular "he" referred to the fact that after his brother's death, Antiochus alone was left to carry on the struggle with the Ptolemies.

The purpose of the war against Ptolemy was to recover Syria from Egyptian dominion; and after a series of campaigns, Antiochus did succeed in bringing the land back under his control. When this verse says that he would "keep on coming and overflow and pass through, that he may again wage war up to his very fortress," it means that after an initial defeat, Antiochus would mount a second expedition to enter into the strongholds of Egyptian power.

In their first battle, Ptolemy marched into Syria with an army of 70,000 soldiers, 5,000 horses, and 73 elephants. He was met by Antiochus's army of 62,000 soldiers, 6,000 horses, and 102 elephants. In the first great battle, Antiochus was defeated. However, in fulfillment of this prophecy, Antiochus returned the next year to rout the Egyptian army. He invaded Syria from Antioch and subdued it along with Palestine and Gaza.

Verse 11: When the king of Syria reclaimed his old territory, the king of Egypt was moved to anger. Thus we read, "The king of the South will be enraged and go forth and fight with the king of the North." There were almost constant battles between the two countries.

Here the "king of the South" was Ptolemy IV Philopator of Egypt. He met Antiochus the Great at the Battle of Raphia and forced him to retreat once again to Antioch. After this notable Egyptian victory, cities in Syria and Palestine hastened to declare their submission to Ptolemy Philopator. They preferred Egyptian rule, under which they had long been, to the rule of Syria. Had Ptolemy been the right kind of king, he could easily have retained control over these lands.

Verse 12: After the multitudes of the king of the north were given into the hand of the king of the south, what would happen? The Angel told Daniel, "His heart will be lifted up."

When Ptolemy Philopator defeated Antiochus, he began to display pride and self-confidence. He was naturally lazy and profligate, and he gave himself over to the indulgence of his every desire. The reason for his great pride was his successful conquest of Syria.

After his victory, Ptolemy gave himself up with abandon to a life of luxury and licentiousness. He began to lose the allegiance of his own subjects because of his conduct. He was viewed with growing disfavor, and when he failed to press his advantage over Antiochus of Syria, his own people revolted against him. It is one of the paradoxes of history that Ptolemy Philopator was much less popular after his successful war against Antiochus than he was before it.

Verse 13: Despite his earlier defeats, the king of the north "will again raise a greater multitude" and seek to reclaim Syria from the king of the south. We read that "after an interval of some years he will press on with a great army and much equipment." King Antiochus of Seleucia was to return to wrest from King Ptolemy of Egypt control of the lands of Syria and Palestine.

This prophecy was fulfilled in 203 B.C., some fourteen years after the previous war. Antiochus had conquered the Parthians and other eastern peoples in the interim, and he used the wealth procured by those conquests to finance his newest campaign into Syria. Secular history verifies every statement made in this chapter and confirms every detail of these predictions, which were made long before the events actually occurred.

Verse 14: Antiochus the Great was not the only one who opposed the king of Egypt; others, such as King Philip V of Macedon, did as well. Antiochus and Philip agreed to invade Egypt, whose king was now Ptolemy V Epiphanes, and divide the land between them. At the same time, a domestic conspiracy against Ptolemy was foiled by the vigilance of his prime minister.

The Angel now told Daniel what the people of Israel would do during these events. "The violent ones among your people," he said, "will also lift themselves up in order to fulfill the vision, but they will fall down." We must bear in mind that throughout these wars between Syria and Egypt, the people of Israel were sometimes under Egyptian domination and sometimes under Syrian domination, since Palestine was usually the scene of their struggle.

Ptolemy IV Philopator had conquered Coelo-Syria and Palestine, and Ptolemy V Epiphanes inherited them when he came to the throne. However, the Angel revealed to Daniel that some Israelites, because of Ptolemy's weakness, would attempt to overthrow his rule in Palestine and reestablish their own independence. They decided to shift their support from Ptolemy to Antiochus.

The ancient historian Flavius Josephus describes the fulfillment of this prophecy: "The Jews, of their own accord, went over to him and received him into the city [Jerusalem] and gave plentiful provision to his army and to his elephants, and readily assisted him when he besieged the [Egyptian] garrison which was in the citadel of Jerusalem." Josephus went on to say that Antiochus showed many favors to the Jews and commended them for their actions, all the while deferring to their religious scruples.

The Angel told Daniel that all this would be done "in order to fulfill the vision." In other words, the Israelites would fulfill all that had been foretold concerning them, not by their own design but as a natural result of the actions of the kings of the north and the south. When the Angel went on to add, however, that "they will fall down," He meant that the goal the Israelites hoped to achieve would not be realized. They would not succeed in freeing themselves from Egyptian domination, nor would they gain political independence. When Antiochus returned to Palestine from his campaign into Egypt in 198 B.C., he slew many of the Jews who had favored Egyptian rule and who had aided Ptolemy's cause. On the other hand, the Jews who had obeyed the Law of Moses and had not joined the coalition against Antiochus were not punished but granted even greater favor.

Verse 15: In 198 B.C., Antiochus the Great returned to Palestine. He conquered the Egyptian army at Paneas, took Sidon and Patara, and made himself master of the entire region. Ptolemy had sent General Scopas to hold Palestine under Egyptian domination, but Scopas was defeated by Antiochus.

We read in this verse, "The king of the North will come, cast up a siege mound, and capture a well-fortified city." When Antiochus defeated Scopas at Paneas, the Egyptian general fled and entrenched himself in the city of Sidon. Antiochus pursued him there and laid siege to the city. Further, "The forces of the South will not stand their ground, not even their choicest troops, for there will be no strength to make a stand." King Ptolemy sent a choice army, led by three select generals, to rescue Scopas. It was too late, however; the siege of Sidon reduced the city by famine, and Scopas was forced to surrender. In all these details, the fulfillment of these prophecies is confirmed by history.

Verse 16: "But he who comes against him will do as he pleases": this means that Antiochus would be completely successful in his campaigns against Ptolemy. He had his way against his enemy, "and no one will be able to withstand him." Neither Scopas nor the three generals sent to rescue him—Eropus, Menocles, and Diamoxenus—would be able to stand before Antiochus.

Following his victory over the king of the south, the king of the north "will also stay for a time in the Beautiful Land" of Palestine. Antiochus would take possession of the Holy Land, and no one would be able to resist him. He would stay "with destruction in his hand." The destruction referred to here was that which always results from the carnage of warfare. No special destruction was intended, since Antiochus actually favored the Jews and granted them special privileges. But when war ravages the land repeatedly, great destruction must result, even in the absence of wanton vandalism.

Verse 17: Antiochus, flushed with his success against Egypt, would seek to extend his victories even further. He actually determined to invade Egypt itself, but the plan was never carried out, for he was engaged in wars in Asia Minor. However, he did marshal all the forces at his disposal, with the intention of dethroning and humiliating his Egyptian rival.

Antiochus was to bring to Egypt "a proposal of peace which he will put into effect." Some translate this "proposal of peace" as "upright ones," in the sense that perhaps Antiochus would align himself with some of the Hebrew people in order to take advantage of every favorable condition.

Antiochus's daughter, the famous Cleopatra, was given in marriage to an Egyptian prince. It was the old scheme of international politics in which a marriage is contracted to cement political relationships. This was in fulfillment of the prophecy that "he will also give him the daughter of women." Antiochus had hit on this plan because he was now at war with the Romans as well and needed to use his armies against them.

Antiochus had to be sure that Egypt would not join the Roman forces against him, and its neutrality could best be assured by just such a marriage of convenience. Thus, Cleopatra was given in marriage to Ptolemy V Epiphanes, son of Ptolemy IV Philopator. The Egyptian prince was then thirteen years of age.

Ptolemy was swayed by a weighty consideration: the dowry given by Antiochus was no less than Coelo-Syria, Samaria, Judea, and Phoenicia. The marriage took place in 193 B.C. Cleopatra was designated here as "the daughter of women" because her position would be preeminent among the women in her land.

Why should Antiochus marry away his daughter to his greatest enemy? "To ruin it," the passage says. Some take this passage to mean that Antiochus filled Cleopatra with evil schemes to bring Egypt under his sway; still others think that she was meant to neutralize any attempted alliance between Egypt and Rome against Syria. In fact, Antiochus the Great had both purposes in mind. Finally we read, "She will not take a stand for him or be on his side." Antiochus's scheme boomeranged, when Cleopatra became more attached to her new Egyptian husband than she was to her Syrian father.

Verse 18: When Antiochus the Great of Syria went to war against the Romans, he turned "his face to the coastlands and capture[d] many" islands of the Mediterranean Sea, especially those near Greece. This war, which lasted from 193-190 B.C., ended in the defeat of Antiochus at Magnesia (near Ephesus). It resulted in the subjection of Syria to Rome as a Roman province; although Syria was still permitted its own kings, they had become vassals of Rome.

We read here that "a commander will put a stop to his scorn against him; moreover, he will repay him for his scorn." Antiochus had indeed captured many islands in the Mediterranean, yet a Roman commander was ultimately able to defeat him and restore Rome's honor. He was Lucius Cornelius Scipio, brother of the famous Scipio Africanus. Through Scipio, the scorn that Antiochus had heaped upon the Romans would rebound on his own head. Once again, the testimony of history confirms every detail of these prophetic Scriptures.

Verse 19: Beaten back on every front when he attacked the Romans, Antiochus finally decided to return home and seek the protection and security of his own fortresses. He attempted no further campaigns of conquest, but was content to seek security in his own dominions. That was the fulfillment of the first part of this verse, which predicted that he would "turn his face toward the fortresses of his own land."

The second part of the verse states, however, "He will stumble and fall and will be found no more." Antiochus attempted to plunder a temple in Elam. This arrogant sacrilege so angered the people that an insurrection against him erupted, in which the king and his guards were all killed. Thus came Antiochus the Great to an ignoble end.

Here, too, end the prophecies concerning Antiochus the Great; the details and particulars of his reign, conquests, and wars are as accurate as if they had been written after the event. This entire account is just what one would have expected, not of a prophecy before the fact, but of a record after the fact.

Verse 20: This new paragraph of Scripture marks the beginning of a new train of thought. The prophecies about Antiochus the Great having been concluded, we now turn our attention to his successor.

The man who arose in the place of Antiochus the Great as king of Syria was Seleucus IV Philopator, who reigned from 187-175 B.C. This verse predicted that "in [Antiochus's] place one will arise who will send an oppressor through the Jewel of his kingdom." The word "oppressor" could also be translated "an exactor of tribute"; this new king would distinguish himself by using every means at his disposal to extort tribute from his people. When this verse states that he would go "through the Jewel of his kingdom," it meant that he would lay the richest parts of the realm under tribute.

The purpose of this taxation is not stated. It could have been for the payment of debt, for purposes of war, for a luxurious court, or for purposes of display. We do know that Philopator was indebted to Rome; he had to pay the tribute imposed when his father was defeated at Magnesia. A large portion of this tribute had to be raised from the Jews living in Palestine.

"Yet within a few days," warned the Scripture, "he will be shattered." This successor's reign would be relatively brief compared to that of Antiochus. In fact, history records that Seleucus Philopator ruled for only eleven or twelve years, compared to the thirty-seven-year reign of Antiochus. He died "neither in anger nor in battle": his death would come about neither through the revolts of his people nor through the wounds of war. In this particular, too, Philopator fulfilled the prophecies of Scripture. For unlike his predecessors, he died by the hand of his own minister, Heliodorus, who poisoned him.

Verse 21: From verses 21 through 35, an extended portrait is painted of that dread and treacherous king who has often been called "the Antichrist of the Old Testament." We were first introduced to him in the eighth chapter of the book of Daniel, where he was known as the "rather small horn" (Dan. 8:9-12). This man opposed both the people of God and the worship of God with a diabolical venom and hatred. His name is rightly despised by Jews throughout the world, for many were his atrocities, and nothing was too atrocious for him to carry out.

After Seleucus IV Philopator died, his younger brother used the support of the king of Pergamum to take advantage of the unsettled conditions and usurp his throne. He quietly ascended the throne and was crowned Antiochus IV in 175 B.C., while the rightful successor—Philopator's heir, Demetrius—was in Rome. His flattering courtiers called him Antiochus Epiphanes, "the illustrious" or "magnificent one"; his enemies called him Antiochus Epimanes, "the madman."

The Scriptures call Antiochus Epiphanes "a despicable person." That epithet applies equally well to him both as a ruler and as a man. In every respect, he was a low, vile person; and he demonstrated this repeatedly, both before and after he became king of Syria. One writer described him in this way:

He often lounged like a mere idler about the streets of Antioch, attended by two or three servants, not deigning to look at the nobles. He would talk to goldsmiths and other mechanics in their shops; engage in idle and trifling conversations with the lowest of the people; and mingle in the society of foreigners and men of the vilest character. He was not ashamed to go in the dissipated circles of the young; to drink and carouse with them; and to assist their merriment by singing songs and playing on his flute.

Other, equally unbecoming characteristics were ascribed to him as well.

This verse referred to the new king as one "on whom the honor of kingship has not been conferred." This was a prediction that Antiochus Epiphanes' coronation would not be justified by any law, act of the nation, or legitimate claim to succession. Antiochus came "in a time of tranquility" and gained the throne without show of arms. He carried through his scheme when no one expected it, when the people would be caught off guard. No one entertained the thought that Antiochus would try to succeed to the throne upon the death of his brother; everyone assumed that his purpose in returning to Syria from Rome was to unseat the usurper Heliodorus and give the throne to his nephew Demetrius, the legal heir.

However, this verse predicted that Antiochus would "seize the kingdom by intrigue." The means he employed to attain his goal were deceit and promises to the king of Pergamum that Syria would back his cause. Since he had lived in Rome for many years, Antiochus may have promised aid from the Romans, as well.

Verse 22: We read here, "The overflowing forces will be

flooded away before him and shattered, and also the prince of the covenant." The picture we get here is one of a forceful, sweeping invasion of some country. It has been suggested that the invaded land could be either Palestine or Egypt.

The latter is more probable in light of Antiochus's alliance with the king of Pergamum. This invasion was one of his first acts as king.

Who was the "prince of the covenant"? This probably did not refer to the high priest of Israel, because he was not known by that title. Instead, it is more likely that "the prince of the covenant" referred to the king of Egypt, Ptolemy VI Philometor, with whom Antiochus had signed a treaty.

Verse 23: This treaty between Antiochus Epiphanes and Ptolemy Philometor was intended to settle their dispute over Palestine Coelo-Syria, which repeatedly had been passed between them in the course of their struggles.

When this verse prophesied that "he will practice deception," it referred to the fact that Antiochus never intended to adhere to the terms of his treaty with Ptolemy, nor would he abide by its provisions. On the contrary, he exhausted every possible means of evading the terms of the treaty; whereupon he finally launched a series of bloody wars against Egypt. Throughout this entire process, Antiochus offered repeated protestations of friendship to Ptolemy—even while he plundered the Egyptian countryside.

To perform his deception, Antiochus first went to Egypt "with a small force" of troops, as though he were paying Ptolemy a friendly visit of state and trying to help settle the young king on his throne. On the way, Antiochus took town after town until finally Ptolemy himself was completely in his power.

Verse 24: With craft and cunning the king of the north would enter Egypt and suddenly, in a time of security and peace, lay hold of the best parts of the land, from Memphis to Alexandria. These were the most productive, most fertile portions of the whole land of Egypt.

None of Antiochus Epiphanes' ancestors had been able so cleverly and completely to conquer Egypt and take so much plunder. The previous wars that Antiochus's ancestors had waged against Egypt had been fought in Palestine and Coelo-Syria. Thus, we read it prophesied here that "he will accomplish what his fathers never did, nor his ancestors."

We read further in this verse, "He will distribute plunder, booty, and possessions among them, and he will devise his schemes against strongholds, but only for a time." When Antiochus successfully invaded Egypt, he rewarded his followers with the spoils he had taken. He made his great strikes against the most important strongholds of Egypt so that with each victory he became stronger and more entrenched in the land, until at last he made the king of Egypt a virtual prisoner—but "only for a time." Antiochus was dislodged from Alexandria by the threats of the Romans, who commanded him to leave Egypt. However, there was another reason to return to Palestine: a false report of Antiochus's death had produced great joy in Judea. When he heard of it, Antiochus resolved in his anger to take revenge upon them, so he left Egypt to subdue Jerusalem.

Verse 25: "And he will stir up his strength and courage against the king of the South with a large army." This evidently referred to a later invasion of Egypt by Antiochus. During the years of his reign, Antiochus Epiphanes invaded Egypt four times, with varying degrees of success. The "king of the South," in this case, was Ptolemy VII Physcon, who was the younger brother of Ptolemy Philometor.

Ptolemy Physcon was trying to usurp the Egyptian throne from his brother, Philometor, whom Antiochus had promised to aid. For that reason, "he will not stand." Physcon was unable to withstand the assaults of Antiochus. His navy was defeated, and Antiochus both kept Memphis and laid siege to Alexandria. We read finally, "Schemes will be devised against him." Plans would be formed by the invading armies for the overthrow of the king of Egypt.

Verse 26: Ptolemy Physcon's own family, trusted friends, and counselors proved unfaithful and treacherous to him, for they betrayed him to the invading Syrian army. When this verse states that "his army will overflow," the meaning seems to be that the army of the usurping king of Egypt would be great and spread itself out over much territory; however, it would not be able to keep out the Syrian invaders. Thus, "many will fall down slain" from the ranks of Physcon's followers.

Verse 27: The two kings referred to here were Antiochus Epiphanes and Ptolemy Philometor, who, when they met, planned united campaigns of conquest, oppression, and robbery. Antiochus was the dominant spirit, but Philometor agreed to his schemes. This verse predicted that "they will speak lies to each other at the same table." Both would enter into agreements without any intention of keeping them.

However, we read, "it will not succeed." Whatever their individual purposes may have been, they did not succeed, for "the end is still to come at the appointed time." Events would unfold in a manner entirely different from what these two kings had planned, for God would overrule every design of their wicked hearts. At God's appointed time, events would unfold according to His will, not theirs.

Verse 28: Even though Antiochus stopped to harass Jerusalem on his return from Egypt, he was on his way back to his own land of Syria, laden with the spoils of his war with Egypt. We read, however, "His heart will be set against the holy covenant." This referred to the people of Israel, who by virtue of their covenant relationship with God are known as "the people of the covenant."

The reason for Antiochus's attack on Jerusalem, as we saw in verse 24, was the joy expressed by the Jews when they heard the false report of his death. When we read that "he will take action and then return to his own land," it meant he was able to accomplish his purpose in Jerusalem. Some historians report that Antiochus took the city by storm, plundered it, and slew 80,000 men, women, and children. He took 40,000 prisoners and sold as many into slavery.

In addition to this, Antiochus entered the sanctuary, robbed it of its vessels of silver and gold, and stole some 1800 talents of gold. Worst of all, he sacrificed a pig on the altar, boiled some of its flesh, and sprinkled the whole Temple with the broth (see 1 Maccabees 1:21-28; 2 Maccabees 5:15-21).

Verse 29: In the wisdom and purpose of God, Antiochus Epiphanes would return "to the south" to invade Egypt once again. He had heard that the two royal Egyptian brothers, Philometor and Physcon, had formed an alliance with Greek troops, whose purpose was to withstand any further interference in Egyptian affairs by Antiochus of Syria.

Now Antiochus determined to take the entire nation of Egypt, to make it part of his empire. However, we read, "This last time it will not turn out the way it did before." The former successes of Antiochus against Egypt would not be repeated, for he would be unable to pierce through the Egyptians' united front.

Verse 30: The chief reason that Antiochus's latest venture failed was that "the ships of Kittim will come against him." "Kittim" undoubtedly referred to the Romans, as is clear from recent discoveries in the Dead Sea Scrolls.

The Romans sent an ambassador to Antiochus to demand that he desist from his attempt to invade Egypt. When the ambassador, Popilius, presented Rome's demand, Antiochus replied that he would refer the matter to his council at home. Popilius drew a circle in the sand around the king and said, "Before you leave that circle, you must give me an answer that I can report to the Senate." In his confusion,

Antiochus consented to the demands of the Roman Senate and left Egypt in peace.

How important is a forthright decision in all matters in life, especially in those that relate to our eternal welfare!

"Therefore he will be disheartened, and will return and become enraged at the holy covenant and take action." Having been so abruptly stymied, Antiochus was dejected and downcast. He abandoned his purpose in Egypt under pressure from the Romans and turned back toward his own land. Because of his extreme frustration, Antiochus sought any occasion to vent his wrath. He needed only the slightest pretext to turn him once more against the Jews in Jerusalem.

On their way back to Syria, a portion of Antiochus's great army was detached to destroy Jerusalem, thus fulfilling the prophecy in this verse that Antiochus would "take action." Just what kind of action he took was already described in our commentary on verse 28.

Antiochus was not indiscriminately destructive, however. This passage had predicted that "he will come back and show regard for those who forsake the holy covenant." A portion of the nation of Israel was willing to cast off the faith of their fathers; they were apostate. The primary reason for this apostasy was their desire to adopt Greek culture and customs, and Antiochus used this portion of Jewish society as a wedge with which to divide the nation.

Verse 31: "And forces from him will arise, desecrate the sanctuary fortress, and do away with the regular sacrifice. And they will set up the abomination of desolation." Antiochus would be able to muster a good-sized force, with which he would wreak his venom upon the Jews. Notice that the sanctuary was associated in this verse with the fortress, as "the sanctuary fortress." This was intended to keep the invading army away from the sacred area.

After he had taken the city, Antiochus ordered the sanctuary polluted and the sacrifice and worship there to cease.

The first book of Maccabees tells of these events very vividly (1 Maccabees 1:29, 37-49—an amazing passage that will well repay one's reading it).

This passage in Daniel had predicted that the king of the north would "do away with the regular sacrifice." As we just saw, Antiochus Epiphanes accomplished this in 168 B.C. by polluting the Temple and the sacred altar. We read further that he would "set up the abomination of desolation." The term "abomination" is used in the Old Testament with reference to idols, which wreak untold spiritual havoc and desolation (cf. Dan. 8; Matt. 24:15).

Verse 32: This verse referred to those Jews who had turned from their traditional faith and had embraced the religion of their idolatrous, heathen neighbors. These "Hellenizers," as they were known, constituted a major faction in Jerusalem.

This verse predicted that "those who act wickedly against the covenant" would be turned to godlessness. Antiochus would lure many of the Jews away by all manner of promises of favor and personal gain. But the people who knew their God were those who were willing to cleave to their God-given faith and worship Him despite all enticements to apostasy.

These godly Jews were exemplified by the Maccabees and their followers. When this verse predicted that these men would "display strength," it meant that they would exhibit great valor and fearlessness. When it said they would "take action," it meant that while relying on the Lord, they would perform magnificent deeds in battle—just as the Maccabees did.

Verse 33: Not everyone was taken in by Antiochus's insincere flatteries. Those who were not convinced to forsake their faith, "those who have insight," had a responsibility to encourage others to remain true to their faith. By their actions they gave "understanding to the many" and encouraged them to defend their land.

Yet the cost of this defense would be high. "They will fall

by the sword and by flame, by captivity and by plunder, for many days." Their attempts would not immediately succeed; many would fall in battle first, and others would be taken captive. We know that the Maccabees did suffer great losses at first, because they refused to defend themselves when attacked on the Sabbath. Later rabbinical rulings permitted defensive warfare, even on the Sabbath. There were many who perished in the flames, as well, when their homes were burned or they were cast into heated brass cauldrons. Finally, this warfare would continue "for many days." The historian Josephus claimed that the fighting continued for three years (see 1 Maccabees 1:59).

Verse 34: The numbers of the Maccabees' followers could not compare to those of the Syrian army; the rebelling Jews were far outnumbered. However, small additions to their numbers were made from time to time, so that eventually they had grown large enough to contend successfully with Antiochus.

This verse goes on to say that "many will join with them in hypocrisy." Some of those who volunteered to fight the Syrians did so for idealistic reasons, but others joined the fight with false hopes of plunder or reward. Unlike Antiochus Epiphanes, the Maccabees did not mislead their followers by flattery. A few men flattered themselves by proposing great things in their own minds, but successful leaders often draw such kinds of men to themselves without desiring to do so.

Verse 35: In the fortunes of war, some of the godly and right-minded in the army would also fall. This would serve "to refine, purge, and make them pure, until the end time." It would test and purify the army of those who were just outwardly committed to the cause of God's people. Those who had joined the Maccabees out of mercenary or otherwise unworthy motives would be eliminated.

When this verse says that this would continue "until the

end time," it meant simply until the end of the war of the Maccabees. And finally, the Angel said, "Because it is still to come at the appointed time." Here was the assurance that God would limit the duration of the Jews' time of testing, and that they would ultimately triumph.

Verse 36: We believe—along with many Christian interpreters—that from this point until the end of the chapter, we are no longer dealing with Antiochus Epiphanes, but rather with the one of whom he was a foreshadowing, namely, the Antichrist. The details of the prophecies in this section cannot properly refer to Antiochus; for just as God gave definite signs and characteristics throughout the Old Testament whereby Messiah could be recognized, so, too, the Word of God has made clear the identity of Antichrist.

The history of the interpretation of this figure is interesting. Some have said that it refers to various systems of government or to cults. Even individuals have been accorded this title, such as Hitler, Mussolini, and Stalin. We believe, however, that in the end times a great political leader will arise as the head of the revived Roman Empire. Scripture refers to this leader as "the little horn" in Daniel 7:8-11 and as "the beast" in Revelation 13:1-8. In alliance with him—but living in Jerusalem—will be the counterfeit messiah, the Antichrist.

The Antichrist will be a person, not just some abstract principle. It is true that the Bible speaks of "the spirit of the antichrist" in wicked men (1 John 4:3). But that makes him no less real than Satan, whose "spirit...is now working in the sons of disobedience" (Eph. 2:2).

The Antichrist will be a religious leader. The world is seeking someone who can give the authoritative last word in religious matters; since it rejects the Word of God, it turns to man for its answers. The atheism, pantheism, materialism, behaviorism, and skepticism of our day are all preparing the way for the coming of Antichrist.

Early in this century, one of those who advocated the Jews' return to Palestine was reported to have said, "We are ready to own any man as our Messiah who will establish us again in the land of our fathers." It is true that the Jews have been restored to their ancestral homeland. Yet that restoration has been fraught with uncertainty, instability, and fear —characteristics that have been attendant to this very hour. Looking ahead, prospects are not rosy: there are trying and difficult days yet to come.

Turning now to the verse at hand, we read that "the king will do as he pleases." Self-will characterizes this figure. He is neither God-directed nor God-prompted; as a result, "he will exalt and magnify himself above every god." This is the distinguishing feature of the Antichrist, self-exaltation, just exactly as is described in 2 Thessalonians 2:4. This self-exaltation will not only deceive Israel, but apostate Christendom as well.

The Antichrist will exalt himself "above every god." He will seek to displace even the idolatrous worship of the heathen. "And [he] will speak monstrous things against the God of gods." His blasphemous statements against God will be unparalleled. He will refuse allegiance to God in heaven and, as the Lord Jesus Christ predicted in John 5:43, he will "come in his own name." Will God permit such defiance, even for a brief time? Yes. We read that he will be allowed to "prosper until the indignation"—the time of great tribulation on earth—"is finished." Finally, we are reassured that all these things are part of the foreordained plan of God. "That which is decreed will be done." All will come to pass exactly as the Scriptures have indicated.

Verse 37: The marginal reading here is better: "And he will show no regard for the God of his fathers." This expression "the God of his fathers" is the usual one in the Old Testament for the God of Abraham, Isaac, and Jacob; the God of the patriarchs; the God of Israel. This is the name for God that is used in the prayer book of the Jews to this very day.

This false messiah not only disregards the God of his fathers, but he also disregards "the desire of women." He will have no room for that One who is preeminently the Desire of women, Messiah Himself. It was the fond hope and longing of Jewish women that they might be the channel through whom Messiah would be born. The reason that Antichrist has no respect for the Desire of women is that he will seek to take that place himself.

Continuing, we read, "Nor will he show regard for any other god." He will set himself above all forms of worship, magnifying himself. He will sit in the Temple of God, claiming to be God Himself. The Antichrist will be endowed with satanic power. He will be able to blind men's minds, causing them to believe in a lie, and he will work signs in confirmation of that lie. Since his purpose will be to counterfeit the Lord Jesus Christ, he will be opposed both to Christianity and to Judaism (cf. Rev. 13:11-18). He will aim to displace the worship of God from all hearts, arrogating that to himself.

The Antichrist will attempt to efface from the minds of men the truth of God. He will do so by claiming (in all probability) to give them something even more advanced. The main purpose of Antichrist is to lead men away from trust and faith in God. What Cain started in the way of self-made, man-made religion, the Antichrist will complete with satanic cunning and power. Just as Jesus Christ is the head of the true church, so, too, the Antichrist will have his false system under him, which Scripture calls "BABYLON THE GREAT, THE MOTHER OF HARLOTS AND OF THE ABOMINATIONS OF THE EARTH" (Rev. 17:5; see 17:1—18:24).

Verse 38: The Antichrist will elevate himself above all gods and objects of religious worship, yet there is one person whom he must respect. After all, the Antichrist, as a religious leader, would be powerless to command men if he had no military arm with which to execute his policies. Therefore, he must pay homage and tribute to the one who is designated as "the god of fortresses." This is undoubtedly the Roman beast, head of the revived Roman empire (cf. Rev. 13:1-10).

The beast in Rome and the Antichrist in Jerusalem will be in league together. The beast, as the political leader, will furnish the military strength needed to keep the Antichrist in power. In exchange for this the Antichrist, as the religious leader, will see to it that the beast is supported with the tribute of "gold, silver, costly stones, and treasures." This mutual alliance will work for the benefit of both.

Verse 39: Having obtained the backing of the powerful head of the Roman empire, the Antichrist will be secure in his dealings with all who might oppose him. The "foreign god" mentioned here is the Roman beast, the "the little horn" described in chapter 7. The Antichrist will reward all who help him with prestige and power, and he in turn will support the claims of the beast. To pay the tribute necessary to his alliance with the beast, the Antichrist will farm out the land.

Verse 40: The remaining six verses of chapter 11 clearly refer to the time of the end, as this verse plainly states. This final section of the chapter is a vivid record of the conflict that is to come in the last days. In those days, the "king of the South" will come against Jerusalem. Then the "king of the North," with whirlwind speed and violence, will sweep down upon him "with chariots, with horsemen, and with many ships." He will penetrate the entire region of the southland.

Verse 41: The king of the north will overwhelm the land of Palestine, as well. The speed of his attack could well catch the beast and the Antichrist off guard. Warfare in our century has depended so much on speed and priority of attack.

For some unknown reason, the king of the north will be unable to conquer the lands of Edom, Moab, and Ammon, all of which lie east of the Jordan. It may merely be an indication of the king's plan of attack, which might not consider these territories as important as the rest of the land.

Verse 42: Wherever he strikes, the king of the north is successful. The king of the south, who began the series of campaigns, will not be able to stand before the victorious armies of the king of the north.

Verse 43: This king will plunder the gold and silver treasures of Egypt and will hold sway over Libya and Ethiopia. It is interesting to notice that in our own day, both Libya and Ethiopia are allied against Israel.

Verse 44: During the end times, in the midst of these sweeping and overwhelming victories, the king of the north will be troubled by tidings out of the east and north. He will turn back from the south, then, to meet the thrust of these enemies. Among them will doubtless be the armies of the Roman beast, as well as those of the "kings from the east" (Rev. 16:12). His fury will grow as he goes forth to meet his enemies' onslaught.

Verse 45: The king of the north will meet his doom "between the seas and the beautiful Holy Mountain." There will be no ally or confederate who will help him; thus, this passage predicts the end of the powerful king of the north. In the book of Revelation, the doom of the beast and the Antichrist is also described (Rev. 19:20).

We are living in days when strong delusion is being spread abroad and diverse teachings are carrying many away. The Word of God tells us, "It is good for the heart to be strengthened by grace" (Heb. 13:9). Christ is the same today for every needy heart; He is waiting to bestow eternal life on any heart that will simply receive Him.

12 The Time of the End

" **N**ow at that time Michael, the great prince who stands *guard* over the sons of your people, will arise. And there will be a time of distress such as never occurred since there was a nation until that time; and at that time your people, everyone who is found written in the book, will be rescued. ² And many of those who sleep in the dust of the ground will awake, these to everlasting life, but the others to disgrace *and* everlasting contempt. ³ And those who have insight will shine brightly like the brightness of the expanse of heaven, and those who lead the many to righteousness, like the stars forever and ever. ⁴ But as for you, Daniel, conceal these words and seal up the book until the end of time; many will go back and forth, and knowledge will increase."

⁵ Then I, Daniel, looked and behold, two others were standing, one on this bank of the river, and the other on that bank of the river, ⁶ And one said to the man dressed in linen, who was above the waters of the river. "How long *will it be* until the end of *these* wonders?" ⁷ And I heard the man dressed in linen, who was above the waters of the river, as he raised his right hand and his left toward heaven, and swore by Him who lives forever that it would be for a time, times, and half a *time;* and as soon as they finish shattering the power of the holy people, all these *events* will be completed. ⁸ As for me, I heard but could not understand; so I said, "My lord, what *will be* the outcome of these *events?*" ⁹ And he said, "Go *your way*, Daniel, for *these* words are concealed and sealed up until the end time. ¹⁰ Many will be purged, purified and refined; but the wicked will act wickedly, and none of the wicked will understand, but those who have insight will understand. ¹¹ And from the time that the regular sacrifice is abolished, and the abomination of desolation is set up, *there will be* 1,290 days.

179

[12] How blessed is he who keeps waiting and attains to the 1,335 days! [13] But as for you, go *your way* to the end; then you will enter into rest and rise *again* for your allotted portion at the end of the age."

Introduction

This last chapter of the book of Daniel is very closely related to the one that preceded it. It concludes the Angel's disclosure of the things that were "inscribed in the writing of truth" (Dan. 10:21), and it indicates Daniel's place in the scheme of God's plan for the ages.

Verse 1: The expression "at that time" refers the reader back to the events described at the end of chapter 11. It has been suggested that the events described here are linked with the war in heaven, which is described in the book of Revelation (12:7-12). In that passage, the archangel Michael is one of the most prominent participants; he is so in this one, also. Michael's antagonist in these struggles is Satan, who is known in Scripture as a relentless enemy of the people of Israel, as well as of all God's people (see Zech. 3:1; Rev. 12:9-10).

As this great "time of distress" begins, what will happen? We read that "Michael, the great prince who stands guard over the sons of your people, will arise." Yes, the great archangel will interpose himself on behalf of the people of Israel to champion their cause against Satan and the forces of evil (cf. Rev. 12:7). It cannot be repeated too often: this passage refers to "the sons of your people," the people of Israel. There is no thought here of the church, which is God's people from all nations of the earth. Unless this vital distinction is kept in mind, havoc will be wreaked in the interpretation of the book of Daniel, as well as other books of the Old Testament.

We are not to understand that Michael has never before

stood to defend Israel, whose special guardian he is; but "at that time" he will interpose himself in a much more clear and open way. He has always been their defender, but when he steps forward to protect Israel this time, Michael will bring to its great climax God's earthly dealings with His people. The expressions used here to describe this time of distress are the key to understanding that this time of trouble will be out of the ordinary and very special indeed.

This verse predicts that Daniel's people will "be rescued." The best way to test whether this prophecy has been fulfilled already is to ask ourselves whether Israel has been delivered from her enemies. It was not true in the time of Nebuchadnezzar; it was not true in the time of Titus; and it is still not true in our present hour. We conclude, therefore, that these events described in chapter 12 must lie yet in the future, in the times described in Jeremiah 30:1-11 and Matthew 24:15-21: in the Great Tribulation.

There will be deliverance, we notice, yet it will not be granted indiscriminately. Not all will be delivered, regardless of their heart condition for the Lord; only those who are "found written in the book" will be saved. This must refer to those who are "recorded for life" because of their trust in God and in Messiah as Savior (Isa. 4:3). It will require more than natural birth to avail in that day; spiritual birth will be the decisive factor.

Verse 2: When we seek to determine the exact time of the resurrection of the Old Testament saints, this verse is of vast significance. In the first place, we understand this passage to refer to a physical resurrection of physical bodies. Whenever the term "sleep" has been used in connection with the dead, whether in the Old Testament or the New, it has been grossly misunderstood and misinterpreted. The Bible never speaks of sleep in reference to the soul, for sleep is not an activity of the soul. Rather, the Bible always speaks of sleep as an activity of the body (see Matt. 9:18-25; Mark 5:35-42).

There has been so much error circulated on the subject of the resurrection that we should deal with it rather fully at this time. There is no Christian system of Bible interpretation that would dare omit the subject of resurrection, either that of Christ, the saved, or the unsaved. It is absolutely essential, not only to the scriptural doctrine of salvation, but also to the doctrine of future things. Regardless of how much has been written on the resurrection in books secular or religious, in the last analysis, nothing would be known for certain apart from the Bible. Nature may rather weakly illustrate the doctrine of resurrection, but the doctrine itself must be found in the Bible, and there alone. Will there, in fact, be a resurrection of the dead? The holy Scriptures alone have the answer, and their clear testimony is that there will be.

Many Christians believe that there will be one general resurrection for all the dead, sinner and saint alike. They claim that the Bible teaches one great resurrection at a single point in time in the future. On the contrary, the Bible actually teaches that there will be two resurrections: one for the saved and one for the unsaved.

Some of those who hold to one resurrection are honest enough to admit that a single, general resurrection is internally inconsistent, and that Pauline doctrine contradicts it. You see, the resurrection of believers takes place along entirely different lines from that of the unsaved, since the saved are resurrected after the model of Christ's resurrection (1 Cor. 15:20-23; Phil. 3:20-21).

In this passage, Daniel 12:2, we have the first mention in the Old Testament of a twofold resurrection. It follows the time of Israel's tribulation, which was described in the preceding verse. We find the distinction between the two resurrections in the terms "these" and "the others." "These" who have believed in the Lamb of God will first be resurrected "to everlasting life"; however, "the others," who have not believed, will then be resurrected "to disgrace and everlasting contempt." The sense of this passage is definitely of two different groupings, or classes, of individuals.

Notice that this passage does not state how much time will elapse between the first and the second resurrection. Luke 20:35 speaks of "those who are considered worthy to attain to...the resurrection from [out of] the dead." This terminology means that there is to be a resurrection at which some are raised and some are not. This expression is used of Christ and the saints, but never of the unsaved.

First Corinthians 15:20-28 relates the resurrection of the dead directly to the kingdom rule of Christ on earth. Moreover, the resurrection is explicitly said to occur in different stages. Immediate succession is not taught in First Corinthians, because so much time has already elapsed between Christ, "the first fruits of those who are asleep" (1 Cor. 15:20), and the company that will rise at His coming (1 Cor. 15:23). The end-resurrection will occur only when Christ has delivered up the kingdom to His Father. In other words, the thousand-year-long kingdom age elapses between the first resurrection of believers and the second resurrection, that of unbelievers. Revelation 20:4-6 also speaks of a first and a second resurrection, with the entire kingdom age of one thousand years intervening. Some in Israel in that day will be raised in the resurrection of the godly, while others will be reserved to experience the resurrection of the wicked, who will undergo the wrath of God.

Verse 3: The "insight" referred to in this verse is spiritual insight, not worldly wisdom. It is stated that among the people of Israel at the time of their great trial, there will be those who will know the will of God and who will be able to turn others to the Lord and to righteousness. They will be used by the Lord to call forth a believing remnant in the end time, and for their perseverance He will reward them with His blessing and glory. Soul-winning is commended by God in any age, and it will be fruitful in that day as well. "The fruit of the righteous is a tree of life, and he who is wise wins souls" (Prov. 11:30).

Verse 4: Daniel was now commanded by the Angel to seal up the words of this prophecy until the end of time. It is clear that that time had not yet arrived during the prophet's lifetime, and thus these divine disclosures remained hidden.

In the book of Revelation, however, the opposite command was given to the apostle John. There an angel told him, "Do not seal up the words of the prophecy of this book, for the time is near" (Rev. 22:10). Why the difference between these two passages? In the age of Daniel, the time of his prophecies' fulfillment lay far in the future. In John's case, however, the believer is portrayed as living in the age of the consummation of God's purposes on earth. In a very real sense, Christians are living at "the end of time"; for when God speaks the word, His program will reach a speedy conclusion (cf. Matt. 24:27). The only reason God has delayed this long is His patience toward us, as Peter told us (2 Pet. 3:9). He wishes to call back more souls from perdition before it is too late. Hence, from the perspective of the New Testament, the "end of time" is always seen as having drawn near; thus, the seal has been removed from prophecy.

We read here, "Many will go back and forth." This has been interpreted by many to refer to great improvements in methods of transportation, such as our own country has seen in the progression from the horse and buggy to travel in outer space. We are of the opinion, however, that Daniel was speaking of his own prophecy and the manner in which it would be sealed until the end time. For when the time draws near for these predicted events to be fulfilled, there will be much perusing of the book of Daniel—a "running through" the book, as the literal Hebrew indicates.

As a consequence, "knowledge will increase." The definite article is used in the Hebrew, specifying that "*the* knowledge" will increase, knowledge of the prophecy before us. Just this very thing has occurred during the last century of prophetic studies; probably more books have been written on prophecy during the last fifty years than were written in the preceding two hundred years.

Verse 5: Daniel's attention was attracted to another place on the banks of a river; it is probably to be identified with the Tigris (cf. Dan. 10:4). He saw two angels, although they were not so named. Their appearance at this point added majesty and solemnity to the vision.

Verse 6: This chapter began with the onset of the Great Tribulation, and now one of the angels asked the man clothed in linen how long it will last.

Verse 7: The answer was immediately forthcoming and was delivered with the greatest solemnity, as though heaven itself were being called to attest the truth of what was to follow. It will be "a time, times, and half a time" before "all these events will be completed." The expression used here to denote the length of the Great Tribulation is the same as that used in Daniel 7:25, where the persecution of the saints by the little horn was predicted. At the end of that time, judgment was to be passed on the little horn. His power, kingdom, and rule were to be taken from him, and he was to be destroyed.

Continuing in this verse, we read that "as soon as they finish shattering the power of the holy people, all these events will be completed." The end will come only when the Messiah of Israel saves the Jewish remnant from the persecution of the little horn. This is an expressive clause that speaks of the violent persecutions the Roman beast will inflict upon the remnant of Israel.

Verse 8: Daniel confessed that there was much of this vision that was not yet clear to him. He realized that trial and affliction were in store for Israel, and he was eager to know how long it would be before they would be fulfilled.

Verse 9: Again, Daniel was told that this information was meant for a future day and must be sealed up for the present (cf. Dan. 8:26; 12:4). In short, all that he was intended to know was already discerned by him.

There is an important principle to be seen here. As the time for the fulfillment of God's prophecies draws nigh, He grants to men greater insight into them than was formerly possible. This explains the oft-repeated question, Why is it that our grandparents' generation did not occupy itself more with matters of prophecy? We infer from this passage that we are living closer to the hour of their fulfillment than they did. Even they grasped more of the prophetic Scriptures than did their predecessors; so we witness progressively greater understanding of the events of the end time as the day of their fulfillment approaches.

Verse 10: In the time of the end, there will be two kinds of people, the righteous and the wicked, just as there are today. Those who are godly are "those who have insight," as we saw in verse 3. Their witness will result in fruit, and there will be many who will be "purged, purified and refined" in the fires of affliction (cf. Matt. 7:16-20; James 1:2-4; 1 Pet. 1:6-7). The understanding referred to here is not that of intellect but that of the spirit; those who have spiritual discernment will understand the unfolding course of events.

Verse 11: In this verse and the next, we find two further prophecies that designate periods of time. From other passages in Daniel and the book of Revelation, it is revealed that the Great Tribulation actually begins when the regular sacrifice is displaced by the abomination of desolation (cf. Dan. 7:25; 8:13; 9:27; 11:31; 12:1; Rev. 12:6, 13-14). That period of time lasts for "a time, times, and half a time," which is equal to 1260 days, or forty-two months (Rev. 11:2, 12:6, 13-14; 13:5).

Nevertheless, this verse mentions 1290 days; why the additional thirty days? They may have been included as the time needed for the Lord Jesus Christ to purge "out of His kingdom all stumbling blocks, and those who commit lawlessness" (Matt. 13:41). The visible coming of the Lord, however, will occur at the end of the 1260 days of the Great Tribulation (Matt. 24:29-30; Mark 13:24-26).

Verse 12: This passage specifies 1335 days, which implies another forty-five days beyond the thirty days just added in the preceding verse. It has been suggested that these additional forty-five days will end in the celebration of the first millennial Feast of Booths, as was predicted in Zechariah 14:16-21. However, this cannot be proved with certainty. The additional days must somehow be necessary in God's economy for the full establishment of Messiah's glorious kingdom on earth, on the throne of David (cf. 2 Sam. 7:16). There are blessings in store for those who will rise at that hour!

Verse 13: The book of Daniel closes with a tender touch concerning the now-aged prophet. He was told to go his way, the way of all flesh. He had lived to see many of his prophecies fulfilled; others lay far beyond the horizon of his day, centuries in the distant future.

When God finally sets into motion the consummation of the ages, Daniel will be among those raised in the first resurrection "to everlasting life" (Dan. 12:2). His body will respond to the Lord's command to "come forth" and enter into eternal life (Isa. 26:19; John 11:43-44). He will then receive his portion and will lose nothing of the reward that was promised him.

Summary

What a beautiful conclusion this was for the man of God whose life was devoted to the Lord! The same man who separated himself to the Lord in the first chapter is the man who was promised an eternal inheritance in the last chapter. No one ever errs when he allows God to make his choices for him; and no man ever loses out when he is devoted to the Lord.

Dr. Bonar penned the following verses, which are a
source of joy for all believers:

I murmur not that now a stranger
   I pass along the smiling earth;
I know the snare, I dread the danger,
   I hate the haunts, I shun the mirth.

My hopes are passing upward, onward,
   And with my hopes my heart has gone;
Mine eye is turning skyward, sunward,
   Where glory lightens 'round yon throne.

My spirit seeks its dwelling yonder;
   And faith foredates the joyful day,
When these old skies shall cease to sunder
   The one dear love-linked family.

To light, unchanging and eternal,
   From mists that sadden this bleak waste,
To scenes that smile, forever vernal,
   From winter's blackening leaf I haste.

Earth, what a sorrow lies before thee!
   None like it in the shadowy past;
The sharpest throe that ever tore thee,
   Even though the briefest and the last.

I see the fair moon veil her lustre,
   I see the sackcloth of the sun;
The shrouding of each starry cluster,
   The threefold woe of earth begun.

I see the shadow of its sunset;
   And wrap't in these the Avenger's form;

I see the Armageddon-onset;
   But I shall be above the storm.

There comes the moaning and the sighing,
   There comes the hot tears' heavy fall,
The thousand agonies of dying;
   But I shall be beyond them all.

Bibliography for Further Study

Anderson, Sir Robert. *The Coming Prince*, 10th ed. (London: Pickering and Inglis, n.d.). Splendid, and especially good in chronology on 9:24-27.

Barnes, Albert. *Notes on the Old Testament (Daniel).* (Grand Rapids, Mich: Baker, 1950 reprint, 2 vols.). Conservative and thorough.

Culver, Robert D. *Daniel and the Latter Days.* (Westwood, N.J.: Revell, 1954). Fine defense of premillennial position in contrast to the amillennial.

Driver, S. R. *The Book of Daniel.* (London: Cambridge U., 1936). Though nonconservative in approach, he has much linguistic and historical help on the text.

Farrar, F. W. *The Book of Daniel in The Expositor's Bible.* (New York: Armstrong & Son, 1895). Weak in predictive elements of the book.

Ginsberg, H. Louis. *Studies in Daniel.* (New York: Jewish Theol. Sem. of Amer., 1948). Emphasizes linguistic and historical areas. Espouses the hypothetical view that the Hebrew of Daniel is a translation.

Gaebelein, A. C. *The Prophet Daniel,* 14th ed. (New York: "Our Hope" Pub., 1911). Premillennial, dispensational treatment by a master of prophetic exposition.

Ironside, H. A. *Lectures on Daniel the Prophet.* (New York: Loizeaux Bros., 1920). Unexcelled in his generation for solid, popular exposition of Scripture.

Kelly, William. *Notes on the Book of Daniel,* 7th ed. (New York: Loizeaux Bros., 1943). One of the most learned and dependable writers in England of the Plymouth Brethren movement.

Lattey, C. *The Book of Daniel.* (Dublin: Browne and Nolan, 1948). In the accepted Roman Catholic tradition, with its weakness on eschatology.

Montgomery, James A. *A Critical and Exegetical Commentary on the Book of Daniel.* (New York: Scribner's, 1927). Apart from the critical bias common to the *ICC* series, this is one of the most valuable of all commentaries in the areas of text, language, history, and especially the ancient versions.

Pusey, E. B. *Daniel the Prophet.* (New York: Funk & Wagnalls, 1885). This work embodies nine lectures given at the divinity school of Oxford University by its Regius Professor of Hebrew. A work of over 500 pages, it is exemplary in its defense of the book against all untenable criticisms.

Stevens, W. C. *The Book of Daniel,* rev. ed. (Los Angeles: Bible House of L. A., 1943). At one time principal of Nyack Missionary Institute, Stevens clearly unfolds the meaning of the text. Those who have had occasion to study his two volumes on the book of Revelation will find the same sane approach.

Walvoord, John F. *Daniel: The Key to Prophetic Revelation.* (Chicago: Moody, 1971). A superior work and easily one of the foremost of recent commentaries.

Wood, Leon. *A Commentary on Daniel.* (Grand Rapids, Mich.: Zondervan, 1973). An able, reverent, recent treatment of the book by a conservative Old Testament scholar.

Young, Edward J. *The Prophecy of Daniel.* (Grand Rapids, Mich.: Eerdmans, 1949). Very helpful in many ways. Unquestionably orthodox, but weak in eschatology because of the amillennial perspective.